DIS

D0679224

FIT, FAILURE,
AND THE
HALL OF FAME

FIT, FAILURE,
—— *and the* ——
HALL OF FAME

How Companies Succeed or Fail

Raymond E. Miles
Charles C. Snow

THE FREE PRESS
A Division of Macmillan, Inc.
NEW YORK

Maxwell Macmillan Canada
TORONTO

Maxwell Macmillan International
NEW YORK   OXFORD   SINGAPORE   SYDNEY

Copyright © 1994 by Raymond E. Miles and Charles C. Snow

All rights reserved. No part of this book may be reproduced or transmitted in any form or by any means, electronic or mechanical, including photocopying, recording, or by any information storage and retrieval system, without permission in writing from the Publisher.

The Free Press
A Division of Macmillan, Inc.
866 Third Avenue, New York, N.Y. 10022

Maxwell Macmillan Canada, Inc.
1200 Eglinton Avenue East
Suite 200
Don Mills, Ontario M3C 3N1

Macmillan, Inc. is part of the Maxwell Communication Group of Companies.

Printed in the United States of America

printing number
1   2   3   4   5   6   7   8   9   10

Library of Congress Cataloging-in-Publication Data

Miles, Raymond E.
   Fit, failure, and the hall of fame : how companies succeed or fail
/ Raymond E. Miles, Charles C. Snow.
      p.   cm.
   Includes index.
   ISBN 0-02-921265-0
   1. Industrial management. 2. Industrial organization.   3. Success
in business. I. Snow, Charles C. (Charles Curtis)
II. Title.
HD31.M436 1994
658—dc20   94-17717
                                                                      CIP

FLORIDA GULF COAST
UNIVERSITY LIBRARY

CONTENTS

Introduction   1

Part One. Why Organizations Succeed   7

Chapter 1. The Process of Achieving Fit   11
Chapter 2. Early Fit: Creating New Recipes for Success   25
Chapter 3. The Modern Transition   44

Part Two.   Why Organizations Fail   63

Chapter 4. The Process of Misfit   65
Chapter 5. Failure to Respond to External Change   70
Chapter 6. Unraveling From Within   83

Part Three. Future Fit:
*   The Twenty-First Century Challenge*   95

Chapter 7. The Network Organization   97
Chapter 8. Triple Fit:
            Network Roles and the Spherical Form   121
Chapter 9. A New Managerial Philosophy:
            The Human Investment Model   141

Part Four.   Dynamic Fit:
*   The Process of Organizational Renewal*   157

Chapter 10. The Process of Corporate Redesign   159
Chapter 11. The Self-Renewing Organization:
            Learning and Teaching Adaptation   169
Chapter 12. From Idealistic Oughts to Economic Musts   186

Endnotes   201

Acknowledgments   209

Index   211

About the Authors   215

INTRODUCTION

"They already have a product coming out that's better than the one we have on the drawing board."

"The average costs in this industry have dropped at least twenty percent while ours have continued to go up."

"The problem is there are new beasts in the jungle, and it's not clear what they are going to do."

"Sometimes I think we are the only ones playing by the old rules."

Statements such as these, reflecting a growing concern with firms' competitive positions, began accumulating in our notebooks in the late 1970s and early 1980s as we talked with managers in boardrooms, plants, offices, executive programs, and so on. Moreover, it was not long before managers' comments moved beyond concern into resentment, often anger, which was even directed at us as we pointed out how some firms were refocusing and reshaping their structures and processes—learning to do more with less.

"I don't care what anyone says, we're moving as fast as we can."

"We are working on quality, costs, and leadership—I don't know what the hell else we can do."

As the decade progressed, anger and resentment slowly began to give way to confusion and frustration, coupled with a growing willingness to rethink what was happening to companies and why. Our experience with one group of managers reflects this combination of frustration and new insights, an experience repeated dozens of times in the last few years.

In an early discussion session in an executive program, we asked the group, "What's going on in your companies today?

Are you doing the things necessary to be successful in the years ahead?" This particular group of executives was highly experienced, and they quickly recited how competition had changed and listed the main solutions that had been offered to resolve their competitive difficulties. However, not a single one of these executives expressed the belief that these solutions would work. One manager summed up the entire group's feeling when she said, "Basically, we're not certain that anything we try is going to work—no matter how much effort we put into it. In the meantime, we'll keep downsizing and hoping that things will get better." Finally, in an attempt to get the discussion headed in a more productive direction, we asked the group to analyze two companies that were highly successful at the time: Wal-Mart and Rubbermaid. Both companies had recently been added to *Fortune* magazine's list of the most admired U.S. companies. Our question was, "What explains each company's success?"

"The key thing," one executive said, "is to have a clear strategy. Wal-Mart, for example, knows exactly who its customers are and what they want—solid merchandise at bargain prices. Wal-Mart's only problem is to find new locations to do it in."

"But," another executive responded, "Rubbermaid doesn't do it that way. Its strategy is based on innovation—staying ahead of the competition with new, high-quality products that cost more but are worth it."

"If it's not strategy," a third executive chimed in, "it's probably structure. Rubbermaid was just a tired old company until it reorganized. Now its various divisions are focused on their own markets and have their own R&D groups."

"OK, but Wal-Mart is even more successful and it's not divisionalized," another person retorted. "It has different regions, but they all do the same thing, and most key decisions are made centrally. In fact, you could argue that Wal-Mart's centralized information system is the key to its success."

"As long as we're brainstorming here, how about people? Both companies pay a lot of attention to their people. They understand that people have to be empowered to respond to customer needs."

"But it's not the same. At Rubbermaid, managers can actually make product-design decisions, while Wal-Mart managers can only suggest ways to make the system work better."

After some more discussion, during which several additional explanations of corporate success were proffered, one executive finally declared, "Look, ladies and gentlemen, I don't think it's any one of these ingredients. It's the box they come in—the whole package!"

What came out of this discussion, captured succinctly by the last manager who spoke, is an important truth about organizational success. Competitive strategy alone does not determine a company's success. Nor does organizational structure, however innovative it may be. Managerial philosophies that emphasize empowerment may be essential but by themselves will not cause success. What every successful company does possess, however, is a mix of these ingredients—organizational characteristics that fit with one another as well as with the company's environment. It is, in fact, the "box" that counts—the whole package of strategy, structure, and management philosophy and processes.

But even with this important insight—that company success is shaped not by particular elements of management but by the way these elements are brought together and related internally and externally—the lesson is only half learned. To complete the lesson, let us return to the same group of managers in our executive program. Building on the momentum of the previous discussion, we asked them to conduct a similar analysis of corporate success but this time for successful companies of a previous era. Specifically, we asked, "Imagine yourself back in the late 1940s and 1950s. The two companies commanding the greatest attention from both scholars and managers at the time are General Motors and Sears, Roebuck. What has caused their long and spectacular success?"

"Well," said one executive (obviously a fast learner), "it must have been the box, the whole package."

"That's right," another noted, "it wasn't just strategy, though both companies understood the idea of being responsive to their customers. Sears wanted to be a small-town store and yet have big-time buying power to keep prices low and quality up. GM wanted to have a car for every pocketbook—products designed for every market segment. Each strategy made a big company small."

"And it wasn't just structure, even though both companies realized that managers who are nearest to the market [the division manager at GM, the store and department managers at Sears] have to make the key operating decisions."

The first executive, now clearly in control of the argument, summarized by saying, "It wasn't just strategy, or just structure, or just empowering people to make decisions; it was the whole package of ingredients that allowed these companies to create and operate large organizations that seemed simple enough for anybody to understand."

"OK then," a colleague asked, "if Sears and GM had it all together, if the box was packed right, why are they struggling so much today? Didn't you say the secret to success was the box— the package?"

"Yes, but maybe that's not the whole answer," the first executive replied. "The answer isn't just that it's the box—the real secret is *knowing* that it's the box."

"What do you mean?"

"I mean that it isn't enough just to have all the pieces in the right package for that company at that time. Management must truly understand the package—what it can and can't do, what it is right for and what it isn't. I think both GM and Sears lost that understanding over the years. At least what they are today and what they are saying aren't anything like what they were doing and saying then."

"Does that mean," another asked, "that today's stars will be tomorrow's failures? Will Wal-Mart and Rubbermaid have as long a run of success as Sears or GM, or will they run into problems sooner—along with the rest of us?"

"I think," the first executive responded, "it all depends on how well they understand their current success and how well that understanding gets assimilated into the organization."

"I think it's more than that," said another. "They have to understand not only what they are doing and why; they have to understand the alternatives—how to repackage, to find a new arrangement that will be effective as times and conditions change."

Clearly, not every group of managers moves as far or as fast as those in the above example. However, we believe that most managers know that their present collection of principles and techniques is not enough to deal with the complexity of today's markets and organizations, and most are searching for a new way of understanding what is happening and why. Moreover, we believe that most managers, at one level or another, know it is not the separate ingredients but the "box" that produces sustained corporate success. Managers are therefore appropriately wary of this year's buzzwords and approaches, even when they are as important as total quality management or as behaviorally sound as empowerment.

In short, we believe that the difficult competitive issues that companies have faced during the last decade and a half can now be brought into sharp focus and hopefully resolved. Enough organizational experimentation and research have occurred for the recipe of corporate success to be written, understood, and effectively utilized. Although success cannot, of course, be guaranteed, managers who grapple with the logic (or lack of it) embodied in the present mix of strategy, structure, and management philosophy in their own companies will begin to see and understand how that logic is modified, even destroyed, by changing one or more of the ingredients of the mix. That is, they will have a much better chance of avoiding the organizational failures so commonly found today.

This book is about the process of achieving an understanding of the fundamental elements of organizational success and failure. It reflects our own realization that even after years of researching, writing, teaching, and consulting about organizational strategy, structure, and process, we had never put all the pieces together in a form that managers could use. This book, we believe, provides the framework managers need to diagnose the weaknesses in their companies' current mix of strategy, structure, and managerial processes and either restore the operating effectiveness of their present form or redesign the total package to meet new demands. Most important, by focusing on the underlying dynamics of success and failure, the framework we offer goes beyond a one-time fix and prepares managers to meet tomorrow's challenges as well as today's.

Virtually all the new insights that we offer managers in this book have come from our observations of their creativity—the innovations managers have made to invent and align strategies and structures in a constantly changing world. This book is an effort to share those insights.

PART ONE

WHY ORGANIZATIONS SUCCEED

Success is not the goal of an organization. The goal is the production of goods and services that are valued by customers and the broader society. Success is the outcome of achieving that goal. Some companies are never successful. Others are successful in the short run. Only a few are successful over long periods of time. Those that flourish in good times and cope well during lean periods—that is, those that demonstrate year after year that they know what they are doing and do it—we call Hall of Fame companies.

As we stated in the Introduction, company success depends on putting together a complete and complementary package of ingredients: strategy, structure, processes, and a managerial ideology that holds these together and gives them meaning. Further, this package of characteristics must be widely understood and disseminated so that it becomes part of the daily behavior of everyone in the organization. We call this process "achieving fit."

In Chapter 1, we discuss the concept of fit. We describe the external fit between the firm and its environment, and the internal fit of organization structure, management systems, and managerial ideology to a chosen strategy. More important, however, we examine the dynamics of fit. Our contention is that "minimal fit" is necessary for a company to survive, "tight fit" frequently results in excellence and accolades of admiration, and "early fit" may enable a company to be a candidate for the mythical corporate Hall of Fame—an imaginary place of recognition for those firms that sustain unusually high levels of performance over an extended period of time. (Of course, some firms never achieve fit and even Hall of Fame companies, like outstanding athletes, may suffer downturns in performance. We reserve our discussion of "misfits," which usually fail, for Chapter 4.)

Chapter 2 discusses the companies that pioneered the major organizational forms that have appeared over the past hundred years or so. Key historical developments are traced from the time when Carnegie Steel pioneered the functional organization, through General Motors' (and other companies') development of the divisional organization, to TRW's role in the creation of the matrix organization. In each case, the creation or early use of a new organizational form gave the pioneering company a competitive advantage that was difficult to overtake and therefore was long lasting.

Today's successful companies are discussed in Chapter 3. These companies, described in the business press as "winners," "most admired," and so on, include General Electric, Wal-Mart, and Rubbermaid. They have assembled effective organizations from the beginning or have reengineered themselves to be strong competitors—in each case by using a modern version of a traditional organizational recipe. In addition, many of today's successful companies are using the newest form of organization, the network.

CHAPTER 1

THE PROCESS OF ACHIEVING FIT

How does a successful company go about putting together its particular package of essential organizational ingredients? What's involved in devising an effective strategy, organizing to pursue that strategy, and so on? There are no simple answers to these questions. If success were simply a matter of connecting the dots in the right order, there would be many more world-class companies than there are today.

Nevertheless, over the course of business history, many companies have achieved continued success—enough, in fact, to reveal a pattern in how success develops. To understand this pattern, we believe it is useful to think of success as achieving fit. Fit is both a state and a process. That is, if one were to take a snapshot of a successful company at any given point in time, the picture would show a strong external fit between the company and its environment. As a result, customers, securities analysts, community officials, and other constituents would speak highly of the company's products and services. In short, one could say that such a company had a good "strategy."

The same snapshot would also show a strong internal fit; that is, the organization's structure, processes, and managerial ideology would support the firm's strategy. The picture would exhibit great clarity, reflecting the fact that inside the organization everything was working smoothly.

Organizations, however, do not stand still, so the challenge of achieving fit is best conceptualized as a journey rather than as a destination. Our view of the process of fit has several markers along the way, labeled "minimal," "tight," and "early." In this chapter, we will describe each type of fit and illustrate each with company examples. Further, we will describe how the internal and external aspects of fit, properly communicated and understood throughout the organization, turn complexity into simplicity. Last, we will extend the notion of simplicity to the asset of people—what their essential role is in an organization and how they should be managed.

STRATEGY:
ACHIEVING FIT WITH THE MARKETPLACE

The process of achieving fit begins, conceptually at least, by aligning the company to its marketplace—by finding a way to respond to or help shape current and future customer needs. This process of alignment defines the company's strategy. Over time, successful firms relate to the market and the broader environment with a consistent approach that builds on their unique competencies and sets them apart from their peers.

Some firms achieve success by being first, either by anticipating where the market is going or by shaping the market's direction through their own research and development efforts.[1] We call these firms "Prospectors" because they continually search for new products, services, technologies, and markets. In the electronics industry, for example, Hewlett-Packard has been widely recognized as a Prospector for most of its history.

Other successful firms move much less quickly. Instead, they study new developments carefully, wait until technologies and product designs have stabilized, and then apply their competence in developing process efficiencies that will allow them to offer a standard product or service of high quality at a low price. We call these firms "Defenders." Defenders usually do not attempt to operate across a wide product or service arena. Instead, they search for economies of scale in those areas that are relatively healthy, stable, and predictable. By the time Defenders have come on line, most Prospectors have already moved on to

Table 1–1
BUSINESS STRATEGIES AND ORGANIZATIONAL CHARACTERISTICS

Organizational Characteristics	Defenders	Prospectors	Analyzers
Product-market strategy	Limited, stable product line	Broad, changing product line	Stable and changing product line
	Cost efficiency through scale economies	Product innovation and market responsiveness	Process adaptation, planned innovation
	Market penetration	First in to new markets	Second in with an improved product
Research and development	Process skills, product improvement	Product design, market research	Process and product adaptation
Production	High-volume, low-cost specialized processes	Flexible, adaptive equipment and processes	Project development shifting to low-cost production
Organizational structure	Functional	Divisional	Mixed project and functional matrix
Control process	Centralized, managed by plan	Decentralized, managed by performance	Stable units managed by plan; projects managed by performance
Planning process	Plan→Act→ Evaluate	Act→Evaluate→ Plan	Evaluate→Act→ Plan

Adapted from Raymond E. Miles and Charles C. Snow, "Designing Strategic Human Resources Systems"; reprinted, by permission of publisher, from *Organizational Dynamics,* Summer 1984, © 1984. American Management Association, New York. All rights reserved.

new models and applications. They know they have neither the inclination nor the competence to compete with Defenders once the competitive game has focused on the cost-efficient production of standardized offerings.

Successful Prospectors and Defenders are both innovative but in different ways. Prospectors are especially innovative in developing new technologies and products, while Defenders are innovative in delivering an existing line of products and services to their customers. In the computer industry, National

Semiconductor follows a Defender strategy, focusing narrowly on efficient chip production utilizing advanced process technology, whereas Intel Corporation is a leader in product innovation.

If Prospectors succeed by moving fast, and Defenders by moving efficiently, a third group of firms succeeds by doing both in a carefully conceived manner. This type of firm, which we call the "Analyzer," succeeds by being the "second mover" or "fast follower." Most Analyzers operate with a base of established products to which they add carefully chosen new products. Analyzers typically do not originate these products but use their process engineering and manufacturing skills to make a new product even better and their considerable marketing skills to sell it. Matsushita is known for pursuing this strategy in the global consumer electronics business.

Markets are seldom static. They are constantly on the move as tastes change and advanced products and services raise expectations. Prospectors push an industry into new territory, and Defenders help an industry to remain efficient and cost-conscious, making sure the customer gets the most for the least. Analyzers keep both Prospectors and Defenders alert—forcing Prospectors to continue to innovate by matching some of their best offerings at a lower price and forcing Defenders to make new investments in efficiency by approaching their price levels with goods or services of more advanced design. Healthy industries tend to be populated with companies pursuing these different but complementary strategies.

In most industries, during the stable periods between transitions, major companies pursue their own strategies within a comfortable market segment. However, over time, firms may choose to modify their strategies. Prospectors that grow very large—General Motors in the 1960s, for example—may become more like Analyzers. Similarly, some Defenders run out of room in a given product or service area and begin to branch out, also appearing to act more like an Analyzer. Wal-Mart may be headed in this direction, having moved into membership stores and Hypermarts in addition to its standard stores.

Thus, competitive strategies may be modified and even changed. Such shifts, however, are seldom smooth or easy. Externally, a change in competitive strategy may disrupt the industry, and internal changes are never painless. Consequently, unless a firm is alert and adept, today's fit becomes tomorrow's misfit. A company's strategy, or external alignment, must be constantly monitored and periodically evaluated. Everyone in the organization must believe that the strategy is sound and that it will hold up in the foreseeable future.

FITTING ORGANIZATIONAL STRUCTURE AND MANAGEMENT PROCESSES TO STRATEGY

Developing a strategy that fits the marketplace is a necessary ingredient in the organizational "package" of successful firms, but it is far from sufficient. It can only be implemented and sustained by pulling together the necessary resources—people, equipment, money, and so forth—and by arranging these resources in a form that facilitates rather than impedes the chosen strategy.

For example, Prospectors make heavier investments in research and development than Defenders, who in turn tend to invest more heavily in special-purpose equipment than either Prospectors or Analyzers. Moreover, a strategy that depends on responsiveness and innovation generally requires an organization whose rules and rewards focus on results rather than procedures. Conversely, companies attempting to succeed through long-term cost efficiency need to tie operations together with plans and systems that incorporate scale and experience into standard operating procedures.

In general, structure and process ingredients come in only a few generic packages. Three are widely used, though they are not always well understood by the managers who operate them. These are the functional, the divisional, and the matrix organization. A newer organizational form, the network, is still developing. We will discuss these forms, especially their strengths and limitations, in later chapters, but it is useful here to describe them briefly and illustrate how they are linked to different types of strategies.

The functional organization arranges human resources by functional specialty—manufacturing, marketing, finance/accounting, underwriting, customer service, and so forth—and then coordinates their specialized outputs by centrally devised plans and schedules. Most firms pursuing the efficiency-oriented Defender strategy utilize some version of a functional organization. Wal-Mart, for example, integrates functional specialists with a state-of-the-art information system to produce huge logistical efficiencies.

The divisional organization groups a collection of nearly self-sufficient resources around a given product, service, or region: the Jeep/Eagle Division, information technology consulting, southwest region, and so on. Firms pursuing the first-mover or Prospector strategy usually use a structure that allows self-contained groups substantial operating autonomy. As a Prospector, Rubbermaid focuses each of its operating divisions on a particular market segment and expects it to deliver 25 percent or more new products every three years.

The matrix organization is a structural hybrid that overlays program groups or project teams on centrally controlled groups of functional specialists. It is common to find firms that pursue an Analyzer strategy adopting the matrix structure to allow them to shift resources back and forth between project teams and functional departments as new products, services, or programs are brought on line or selected for exploration. IBM for years ran a complex, successful multinational matrix linking product and functional specialists with regional sales and service operations.

The network organization uses market and electronic mechanisms to link together independent specialist firms arrayed along the value chain—manufacturers, suppliers, designers, distributors, and so on—to produce products or offer services. This organizational form can support a variety of competitive strategies under particular circumstances. Nike, the running-shoe giant, uses a largely stable version of the network structure. Dell Computer's network is much more changeable. Still another form of the network organization can be found at ABB Asea Brown Boveri.

At this point, it may appear that corporate success hinges on managers correctly making a few key decisions. First, they need to select a competitive strategy from the menu of generic approaches such as Prospector, Defender, or Analyzer. Then the appropriate organizational structure—functional, divisional, matrix, or network—needs to be fitted to the chosen strategy. As logical as this decision-making process sounds, however, achieving external and internal fit has eluded many companies. In the 1950s, for example, Chrysler Corporation set out to match General Motors model for model in every market, but it did not sufficiently alter its centralized, functional organizational structure. Without the full and independent resources needed to respond quickly to consumers' desires, Chrysler's several automobile lines were not able to keep pace with GM's design and distribution abilities. In the 1970s and 1980s, government deregulation decisions forced numerous trucking, banking, and telecommunications companies to become more "market driven." However, in some cases such as AT&T, it took years of reorganizing to come up with structures and management systems appropriate to a new competitive strategy.

Even when firms adopt a form of organization that is suited to their competitive strategy, they may not complete the fit by adopting all of the logically required management processes. For example, many general managers in various divisionalized firms have been told, in effect, "You're in charge of your division, so run it your way. However, all capital expenditures have to be approved by corporate headquarters." Or, "Get the costs at your plant below those of our competitors, but don't stand in the way of engineering or manufacturing schedule changes." Such contradictions are all too frequently found in otherwise well-managed companies.

In sum, companies are constantly adjusting their strategies in order to maintain an effective alignment with external conditions. However, managers frequently do not think through the implications of these strategic adjustments for organizational structure and management processes. Therefore, when altered strategies prove ineffective, it may not be because they are ill-conceived but rather because the organization has not been appropriately redesigned internally. On the other hand, all companies make internal adjustments from time to time to solve communication and coordination problems. However, these organizational changes are also often made without considering the impact they will have on the company's ability to carry out its current strategy or adapt to environmental change. In short, strategy, structure, and process decisions must be made in conjunction with one another so that the organizational package has—and maintains—a logical integrity.

THE DYNAMICS OF FIT

Given the difficulty of creating and maintaining strong connections among strategy, structure, and process, it is not surprising that companies differ widely in the degree of fit they have achieved. Some lose or never find fit and may fail as a result. Many achieve only limited fit and survive, but never enjoy real success. A few companies have tight fit and rise to the peak of performance, landing on lists of the "most admired" or "excellent" firms. Even fewer firms achieve a new and unique fit well ahead of their peers—making a new strategy work by creating a new way of arranging and managing resources. The few companies that do find this early, tight fit are potential Hall of Famers.

MISFIT AND FAILURE

One can usually sense, from either within or outside the organization, the degree of fit a firm has achieved. If the lack of

Table 1-2
THE DYNAMICS OF FIT

Misfit.	Failure
Minimal fit	Survival
Tight fit	Excellence
Early, tight fit.	Hall of Fame

internal and/or external fit is sufficient, the firm falls further and further behind its competitors until its advertising becomes desperate, its stores begin to look shabby or they close, managers are replaced, its debt burden drags it under, and so on. Once in a downward spiral, it becomes very difficult to reverse course. Some of these misfit companies are well-known—Penn Central, A&P, People's Express, and Wang Laboratories come quickly to mind—but these highly visible failures are only a small minority of all organizations.

MINIMAL FIT AND SURVIVAL

Most firms experience neither major misfit nor tight fit. Instead, they achieve a limited alignment with the marketplace, a limited fit between their strategy and structure, or both. Firms that achieve only minimal fit struggle to make mediocre returns. Their expenses tend to be high because of heavy coordination costs—the price of making a structure work that wasn't designed for the job. The proportion of "problem solvers" (liaisons, integrators, and troubleshooters) is persistently large, and the time it takes to respond to environmental demands is inordinately long. Almost nothing comes easily in the minimal-fit firm. Hard work may be rewarded, but never by the expected level of success. The minimal-fit firm seems to create its own continuing stream of crises and near disasters.

TIGHT FIT AND EXCELLENCE

In contrast to firms struggling with minimal fit, the much smaller number of companies that achieve tight fit appears to have it easy. Externally, customers are happy with the new product designs or with the high-quality services offered at excellent prices. Internally, things seem to work correctly. Because the structure and processes fit the strategy, resources are located where they ought to be, and information and criteria are available at the point where decisions need to be made. Moreover, troubleshooting and rework are not regularly required. The resources saved by doing work right the first time are available to invest in new activities and/or to improve current practice. Hard work usually pays off, and returns—to the company and its people—are high. Morale and confidence are also high because everyone can see clearly how and why things work as they do. Tight fit squeezes out uncertainty and confusion, and it gives complex processes the feel of simplicity.[2]

ARTICULATING THE RATIONALE OF FIT

One of the key roles of management is to help organization members continue to understand the firm's strategy, structure, and processes. In a firm with tight fit, the task of articulation is easy. The organization has not become laden with bureaucratic procedures or unnecessary units. Therefore, everyone can see clearly how and why things work as they do. Well-understood strategies can usually be captured in a sentence or two, perhaps even in a catchy phrase such as GM's early vision of "a product for every pocketbook" or IBM's "service is our business." Of course, mottos and advertising slogans do not make successful strategies— but widespread understanding and consistent action surely do.

Similarly, tight fit gives complex organizational structures clear tasks and responsibilities as well as decision-making authority. In the tight-fit firm, the new member is quickly oriented, and the "rightness" of the way things are done is apparent. Everyone is a tutor because everyone understands explanations that are consistent, and a set of metaphors, myths, and examples is widely owned and commonly used.

The appearance and feeling of simplicity, as well as the broad understanding of purpose and mechanisms in organizations with tight fit, are strikingly visible to the outside observer. Peter Drucker, for example, was impressed with the clarity of goals and understanding at all levels at Sears and GM when he studied those companies in the 1940s and 1950s, as were Tom Peters and Robert Waterman when they observed "excellent" American firms in the late 1970s and early 1980s.[3] Moreover, the more successful a firm becomes, the easier it is for management to articulate why the organization is effective. We simply get better at telling others—and, perhaps even more important, ourselves—exactly what the operating logic of our organizational package is. This deep understanding is, in fact, "knowing that it's the box." Understanding allows the firm to make strategic adjustments to market shifts and social changes while making certain that changes to one piece of the organization are accompanied by proper changes to the rest.

In the minimal-fit company, on the other hand, managers struggle to articulate its strategy-structure-process package. Strategies employ more words and generate less clarity, largely because past experience has not provided assurance that intended performance will occur. Structures and processes, surrounded by an atmosphere of crisis and confusion, do not lend themselves to easy explanation. Departmental responsibilities are not clear. Second-guessing of decisions is commonplace. Crises occur.

In explaining their organizational package and how it works, managers may have difficulty even when the problem is not caused by the firm's intended strategy or its chosen structure. Difficulty arises when the problem is the lack of fit between strategy and structure. Sometimes, as we will discuss later, this lack of fit occurs because managers themselves have not yet fully grasped the operating logic they are attempting to explain. Perhaps the firm has gradually broadened its service base beyond what the structure can handle by adding more and different people. The structure ought to work, these managers believe, but it may need a bit more tweaking. Or, in other instances, the structural repairs made to solve earlier problems have caused new ones that management has not yet recognized.

After all, many of the ingredients of the overall package—rewards, controls, information systems, training and development programs—are the province of several different departments. In short, management cannot for long create the impression of fit when fit does not exist.

OVERCOMING IDEOLOGICAL BARRIERS

Another common reason that managers find it difficult to communicate the package of strategy, structure, and process their firm is seeking to construct is that some pieces of the framework are at odds with managers' deeply held views about people and how they should be managed. For example, a strategy requiring simultaneous, quick responses in several product areas may never receive the decentralized structure it requires to succeed, because corporate managers cannot bring themselves to grant sufficient decision authority to local operating units. No amount of explanation can make such a glaring incongruity disappear. Conversely, in companies with tight fit, managerial ideologies tie controls, rewards, and leadership style to strategy and structure in a widely understood and accepted manner. The concept of "bringing the university laboratory to the workplace" that underlay the founding of Hewlett-Packard led to a management ideology reflecting collegial values and respect for individual abilities and methods. In turn, it was relatively easy to construct reward systems for creativity and performance that paid off by returning profits directly back to their divisional sources, allowing the latter to engage in unfettered research on new ideas. Ultimately, as we will show in Part Three, a complete organizational package must include a managerial ideology that not only complements strategy and structure but also guides job design, team building, decision-making systems, and so on. In fact, existing managerial philosophies are the most difficult barrier for many firms to overcome as they search for new strategies and structures to meet the challenges posed by tomorrow's markets and competitors.

EARLY TIGHT FIT AND THE HALL OF FAME

Again, we believe that tight fit gives a company a decided competitive advantage. Firms that have it get more done with less and can use their slack resources in various ways to sharpen their approach and maintain their lead. An even larger advantage, however, is enjoyed by those firms that first put together the new strategy-structure-process package demanded by major changes in markets and/or technology. Usually, the firms that make these breakthroughs do so not just by finding new strategies—market opportunities may be visible to many firms—but by being clever and far-sighted in designing new structures and processes that make the required strategies work. Moreover, these new structures and processes may be in conflict with existing managerial ideologies, and managers in the pioneering firms have to work their way through to new views about people and leadership. Thus, a key part of designing and understanding a new organizational package is for managers to grasp and then articulate, to themselves and to others, the new operating logic and particularly the new way of managing people required.

Not surprisingly, because of the fundamental changes required by a new organizational form, competitors usually find it difficult to understand and copy. As a result, firms that achieve early tight fit not only do more with less—often much more with much less—but their lead increases as their competitors struggle with half-hearted or partial imitations that may provide them with limited gains but more likely with frustrating confusion. When the lead becomes large and the track record of accomplishment long and widely acknowledged, a firm, like an outstanding athlete, may well deserve Hall of Fame recognition. However, unlike athletes, who ultimately move beyond their periods of peak physical capability into retirement, some firms with Hall of Fame achievements (but by no means all) appear to be able to adapt to new demands and perform at peak levels almost indefinitely. Others, as we shall see in later sections, discover that fit is fragile and never easy to sustain.

In Chapter 2, we will describe in detail the manner in which Hall of Fame companies have created early tight fit at various points of major market change over the last 100 years or so. In Chapter 3, we will describe some companies that both are currently enjoying tight fit and are perhaps on their way to even greater recognition. We will then use the past and current accomplishments of all these companies to outline a package of strategy, structure, and process that the global economy is increasingly demanding.

CHAPTER 2

EARLY FIT:

Creating New Recipes for Success

In the U.S. economy over the 100-year span from 1880 to 1980, three major periods are easily identified, and the transition to a fourth is currently under way. Each of these periods begins with organizations facing large transitions in their external environment—a combination of social, political, technological, and market changes. In each period, therefore, organizations are challenged to discover new strategies to respond to the new environment and to develop organizational structures and management processes to make those strategies work. Historically, only a few companies lead the way. By achieving early tight fit, these firms enjoy enormous success, become the hallmarks of the period, and create a model for other firms to emulate.

In this chapter, our objective is threefold. First, we will describe the three previous periods as well as the process of organizational invention exhibited by each period's leading companies. Because the main organizational form developed in each of these periods, with appropriate modifications, is still used by many of today's Prospectors, Defenders, and Analyzers, our second objective is to explore in depth the logic guiding each form of organization. Finally, our third objective is to identify and explain the barriers faced by the typical firm in each period as it attempted to duplicate the success of the leading companies. In doing so, we will show how and why the early development of an organizational form gives its originators such a powerful and sustainable competitive advantage.

PERIOD I: THE DEVELOPMENT OF MASS MARKETS (1880–1920)[1]

The first period in the development of large business firms covers the last two decades of the nineteenth century and the first two decades of the twentieth century. This period was defined by the emergence of nationwide markets for standard goods and services and was made possible by the establishment of transcontinental railroads and communications systems. The key to success in this period was the harnessing of technical and organizational competence to achieve efficient mass production.

CARNEGIE STEEL: DEVELOPER OF THE FUNCTIONAL ORGANIZATION[2]

The companies that pioneered the organizational form appropriate for mass production were primarily the railroads and steel producers. For example, Andrew Carnegie, then in his early thirties, left a position with the Pennsylvania Railroad to concentrate on manufacturing steel rails. Convinced that the management methods he and others had developed on the railroad could also be applied to the manufacturing sector, Carnegie essentially started the modern steel business in the United States, and he played a major role in forging the world's first billion-dollar corporation, U.S. Steel (now USX).

At the heart of Carnegie Steel's success was its reliance on centralized management (particularly cost accounting and control) and full vertical integration. Carnegie recognized early the benefits of vertical integration in the fragmented, geographically dispersed steel industry in the latter half of the nineteenth century, and his company integrated backward into the purchase of ore deposits and the production of coke as well as forward into the manufacture of finished steel products. Vertical integration permitted a new fit in the steel industry: substantially larger market areas could now be served much more quickly, efficiently, and profitably.

Table 2–1
EVOLUTION AND CHARACTERISTICS
OF ORGANIZATIONAL FORMS

Period	Market Characteristics	Organizational Form	Key Management Mechanisms
Colonial to 1880	Local/Regional markets	Owner-managed	Direct personal control, close supervision *Management by Exception*
1880–1920	Development of national mass markets	Functional, vertically integrated	Central plans and budgets; departments run by staff specialists *Management by Objectives*
1920–1960	Market segmentation and global growth	Diversified, divisionalized	Corporate goal setting; operating decisions made at division level *Management by Coordination*
1960–1985	Mature markets Consolidation, harvesting	Matrix	Mixed forms combining project teams and functional departments; global forms combining product and area divisions

As one of the leading companies in this period, Carnegie Steel helped to invent the "functional organization," which it supplemented with careful plant design, new transportation logistics, continuous technological improvements, and successful (though very limited) product diversification. Other pioneering companies, however, contributed to the refinement and extension of the functional form. Henry Ford, for example, developed his vaunted assembly line during this period and was able to achieve national distribution of his Model T automobile. Unlike small, owner-managed firms that operated only locally or regionally, the size and complexity of the new mass producers required the use of professional managers. These individuals possessed the skills needed to rationalize the use of the entrepreneur's accumulated resources, increasingly substituting impersonal mechanisms of coordination and control for the owner's direct supervision. The success of the functional organization depended on the contributions of specialized departments (manufacturing, sales, accounting, etc.) coordinated by centrally determined plans, budgets, and schedules. Upper-level managers had to delegate day-to-day operations to department heads and intercede only when a unit fell behind on its schedule or exceeded its budget—an approach that came to be called "management by exception." In addition, management had to develop personnel policies and practices aimed at acquiring and holding on to the stable work force necessary for continuous, efficient production.

A MENTAL REVOLUTION

While the managerial behaviors required by the functional organization do not appear to be demanding by today's standards, they presented a major philosophical barrier to turn-of-the-century managers. Frederick Taylor, the preeminent management consultant of the time, said that for scientific management to work, a "mental revolution" had to occur among managers.[3] For managers accustomed to exercising continuous face-to-face supervision, moving back even as far as the daily or weekly review of production and accounting data was difficult. Managers reared on a philosophy that questioned the competence and commitment of everyone but top executives found it difficult to delegate even the smallest decisions. Those who had learned to view lower-level employees as nothing more than interchangeable parts, to be hired and fired at will, lacked the know-how to build the stable and reliable work force the new form required.

Carnegie Steel, Ford, and the other leading companies of the day managed to work their way through these ideological barriers, and by the end of the second decade of the twentieth century, the strategy-structure-process package referred to as the functional organization was well tested and accepted. By the time World War I broke out in 1914, these companies had been enormously successful for many years.

PERIOD II: MARKET SEGMENTATION AND GLOBALIZATION (1920-1960)

The second phase of American business development runs approximately from the end of World War I through the 1950s. This period was defined by growing consumer sophistication and the emergence of the United States as the world's leading industrial power after World War II. The key to company success in this period was the assemblage of growing marketing and managerial competence into increasingly sophisticated organizational packages. In other words, the leading firms of the period built a new organizational form and learned how to make it work.

GENERAL MOTORS: DEVELOPER OF THE DIVISIONAL ORGANIZATION[4]

The company that initially developed the organizational form appropriate for this period was General Motors. Among the early automobile makers, William C. Durant was one of the strongest believers in the market potential of the moderately priced car. Acting on his beliefs, Durant put together a group of companies engaged in the making and selling of automobiles, parts, and accessories. In 1919, the total combined assets of Durant's General Motors made it the fifth largest company in the United States. Although Durant had spotted a potentially large opportunity and had moved rapidly to assemble a set of companies to take advantage of it, he had little personal interest in further developing the organization he had created.

Indeed, in combining individual firms into General Motors, Durant relied on the organizational approach of volume production and vertical integration that was popular at the time. However, this approach led to little more than an expanding agglomeration of different companies making automobiles, parts, accessories, trucks, tractors, and even refrigerators. An unforeseen collapse in the demand for automobiles in 1920 precipitated a financial crisis at General Motors, which was quickly followed by Durant's retirement as president. Pierre DuPont, who had been in semi-retirement from the chemical company, agreed to assume the presidency of GM. One of DuPont's first acts was to approve a plan devised by Alfred P. Sloan, a high-level GM executive whose family firm had been purchased by Durant. Sloan's plan defined an organizational structure for the fragmented company.

Sloan's organizational scheme, which went into effect early in 1921, called for a general office to coordinate, appraise, and set broad goals and policies for GM's numerous loosely controlled operating divisions. Individually, the general officers were to supervise and coordinate different groups of divisions; collectively, they were to help make policy for the corporation as a whole. Staff specialists were to advise and serve both the division managers and the general officers, and to provide the business and financial information necessary for appraising the performance of the individual divisions and for formulating overall policy. Although most of Sloan's proposals had been carried out by the end of 1921, it was not until 1925 that the original plan resulted in a smooth-running organization. The "divisional organization" allowed GM to diversify a standard product, the automobile, to meet a variety of consumer needs and tastes while maintaining overall corporate financial synergy.

From 1924 to 1927, General Motors' market share rose from 19 to 43 percent. Unlike its major competitor, Ford, which had been devastated by the Depression, GM's profits grew steadily throughout the Depression and World War II. The firm headed into the fifties as the leading automobile manufacturer in the world, and for years was the corporate model for similar structural changes in other large American companies.

SEARS, ROEBUCK: AN ALTERNATIVE APPLICATION[5]

Outside of manufacturing, Sears, Roebuck was one of the earliest users of the multidivisional structure. Since its inception, Sears has twice beaten its retailing competitors to a new strategy-structure-process fit. The first phase of the Sears story began in 1895 when Julius Rosenwald, a consummate administrator, joined Richard Sears, a brilliant merchandiser. Together they built a company catering to the American farmer. The Chicago mail-order plant was a major innovation in the retailing business. Designed by Otto Doering in 1903, this modern mass-production plant preceded by ten years Henry Ford's acclaimed automobile assembly line, and it ushered in the "distribution revolution" that was so vital a factor in early twentieth-century America's economic growth.

More widely known, however, is the second phase of the Sears story, which began in 1924 when Robert E. Wood left Montgomery Ward to join the company. Because farmers could now travel to cities in their automobiles and the urban population was more affluent, retail selling through local stores appeared to be more promising than mail-order sales. Promoted to president in 1928, Wood and his new hand-picked management team moved rapidly to create a nationwide retail organization. Montgomery Ward and other retail chains of the period (e.g., J.C. Penney, Woolworth's) were never able to match Sears' sustained success.

The organizational form developed by Sears bore many similarities to GM's divisional structure, but it was geared toward retailing rather than manufacturing. Whereas GM diversified by product, Sears diversified by geographic territory. Each of the territorial units became full-fledged autonomous divisions with their managers responsible for overall operating results. The Chicago headquarters remained a central office with staff specialists and general executives. Sears' successful recipe was not assembled as rapidly as that of Carnegie Steel or General Motors, but it was achieved ahead of all other competing retailers and gave Sears a competitive advantage that was not seriously threatened until the 1980s.

NEW IDEOLOGICAL VIEWS

Two key changes in managerial ideology were apparent in the views of the early practitioners of the divisional organization. The first was the willingness to attribute competence to a broad segment of current and future middle managers. At General Motors, for example, many division and other unit heads were former company owners whose competence had already been demonstrated. President Wood at Sears, Roebuck was convinced that large numbers of store managers, and the department managers under them, could be trained to deliver on the promise to be "a small-town store with nationwide buying power." In fact, one of the strengths of the divisional form, compared to the functional organization, was its ability to develop new management talent rapidly by offering greater opportunities for involvement in important business decisions.

Complementing the change in view with regard to subordinates' competence was a change in the basic form of management control. That is, if division managers were indeed willing and able to pursue agreed-upon division goals as their own, they could be allowed broad discretion and could be evaluated by bottom-line results rather than day-to-day activities. Peter Drucker, a consultant and academic who worked with most of the leading companies of the 1940s and 1950s, termed this approach "management by objectives."[6]

HEWLETT-PACKARD: EXTENDING THE LIMITS OF THE DIVISIONAL ORGANIZATION

The decentralized divisional organization developed by General Motors and Sears, Roebuck (along with a few other outstanding companies such as DuPont and Standard Oil of New Jersey) flourished in the 1950s in the spotlight of publicity from management consulting firms and from academics such as Peter Drucker. For most companies, however, the divisional organization did not serve as a proprietary advantage but merely as a necessary means of maintaining alignment with a market demanding more diversity. Nevertheless, one outstanding company—a Hall of Fame nominee on many ballots—took this organizational form to new heights in its pursuit of leading-edge technological developments in the electronics industry. That company is Hewlett-Packard. Founded in 1939 by William Hewlett and David Packard, HP is the world's largest manufacturer of precision scientific measurement instruments as well as a major player in the computer business. Historically, the company has been noted for its strong corporate culture and nearly continuous high performance in a very demanding industrial environment.

From the beginning, Hewlett-Packard pursued a strategy that brought the products of scientific research into industrial application while maintaining the collegial atmosphere of a university laboratory. HP concentrated on advanced technology and offered mostly state-of-the-art products to a variety of specialized industrial and consumer markets. A given product line and market were actively pursued as long as the company had a distinct technological or design advantage. However, when products reached the stage where successful competition depended primarily on low costs and prices, HP often moved out of the arena and turned its attention to a new design or an entirely new product. As a company that extended the divisional form to its limit, Hewlett-Packard's technological diversification rivaled General Motors' product diversification and Sears' territorial diversification.

Hewlett-Packard's strategy of technological innovation was supported by an organizational structure and management system that were unparalleled in flexibility. The fundamental business unit was the product division—an integrated, self-sustaining organization with a great deal of independence. New divisions arose when a particular product line became large enough to support its continued growth with the profit it generated. Also, new divisions tended to split off when a single division got so large that the people in it started to lose their identification with the product line. Most human resource management practices—especially those concerning hiring, placement, and rewards—were appropriately matched with the company's structural and strategic decentralization. Although Hewlett-

Packard struggled in the late 1970s and early 1980s, and made some substantial organizational changes, the company continues to be a strong competitor in the 1990s.

EXPORTING THE DIVISIONAL FORM

By the end of the 1950s, the divisional organization had been used to facilitate the strategy of related diversification in products (General Motors), geographies (Sears, Roebuck), and technologies (Hewlett-Packard) through the creation of new divisions to develop or respond to emerging markets. The divisional form also facilitated overseas expansion by U.S. firms in the post-World War II era. Divisionalized firms that had been selling their domestic products through overseas sales offices began to convert their international operations into country divisions, which could design and build goods especially for foreign markets. In such cases, the divisional organization was exported in its entirety—a new market simply meant that a new division was added to the organization.

PERIOD III: CONSOLIDATING AND HARVESTING MARKET GAINS (1960–1985)

Beginning in the 1960s and running through the mid-1980s, the third evolutionary period featured industry consolidation and growing globalization. It was a period defined more by efforts to harvest the gains of the earlier period than by the creation of bold new strategic or organizational innovations. Corporate success came as often through the sale and acquisition of assets as it did from developing or applying them.

TRW SYSTEMS: LIBERATING ITSELF WITH A NEW ORGANIZATION[7]

The divisional form of organization spread throughout American industry in the 1950s and on into the 1960s. The flexibility of the divisional approach allowed companies to pursue market opportunities quickly and effectively. However, as global and domestic demands became more complex, some companies were motivated to resolve the primary difficulty associated with the multidivisional structure, namely, its inefficiency. The laboratory for the next set of organizational experiments was the aerospace industry, and one of the notable firms was TRW Corporation.

At the time, aerospace and electronics firms that did business with the federal government regularly landed contracts that called for the development of sophisticated, one-of-a-kind products, often for military use. Firms bidding for such contracts found it difficult (or impossible) to hire new teams of engineering, scientific, and production personnel for each contract and prohibitively expensive to hold such personnel in an unproductive or underemployed status between projects. A more logical approach, it appeared, was to temporarily "draft" the human resources needed for a given project from the permanent departments that employed them on larger, more standardized, and long-term projects. The permanent departments would continue to acquire and develop key human resources. Then, with careful planning and some minimum amount of slack resources, these departments would both move people to temporary projects as needed and reapply them within the department when they returned.

From 1960 to 1963, TRW Systems (a business unit of TRW Corporation) completed the transition from what had been almost a subsidiary of the United States Air Force to an independent, competitive aerospace company. TRW Systems, along with most other aerospace companies, organized itself into a form that came to be called a "matrix." TRW's matrix had five operating divisions: space vehicles, power systems, systems engineering and integration, electronic systems, and systems laboratory. In each division, there were two main types of managers: operations managers and project managers. Operations managers were in charge of functions such as fabrication and manufacturing. Their main job was to maintain and upgrade human and technical resources in their respective specialties.

Project managers, on the other hand, were responsible for particular projects (e.g., Atlas, Titan, Saturn). Their job was to coordinate the resources needed by their project as well as to work directly with the government and private customers. Over time, people and other resources flowed back and forth among projects and functions within the operating divisions.

DIFFUSION OF THE MATRIX FORM

A matrix organization essentially captures in a single structure the best features of the functional and divisional structures. In short, a successful matrix is both flexible and efficient. As the matrix organization became increasingly sophisticated and refined in the 1960s, it spread from aerospace to other businesses. Prominent companies that were heavy users of the matrix organization were Texas Instruments (electronics), Digital Equipment (computers), Citibank (retail banking), and Procter & Gamble (consumer products). These and other companies developed their matrix organizations in the 1960s and used them throughout the 1970s and into the 1980s.

The extension of matrix management to multinational companies began in earnest in the 1980s. In the international arena, matrix organizations were used to integrate products, functions, and markets (regions of the world). For example, large multinational companies such as Philips (Dutch), Matsushita (Japanese), and IBM frequently would link worldwide product divisions, national or regionally based marketing groups, and strategically located manufacturing units to achieve global efficiency as well as local responsiveness.

MATRIX MANAGEMENT IDEOLOGY

The matrix form of organization took a considerable amount of resource-allocation decision making out of the hands of higher-level executives and turned it over to a shared decision-making process among various operating units. This matrix decision process came to be called (sometimes derisively) "management by committee." Thus, while the functional organization demanded that top managers give up personal control over operating inputs and procedures, and the divisional organization demanded that they give up direct control of operating decisions altogether, the matrix organization went a step further. Higher-level executives not only decentralized operating decisions to various units but also allowed those units to transfer and refocus assets across unit lines without direct corporate control.

In successful matrix organizations, managers developed a sophisticated view of subordinate capability and motivation. This view included (1) a growing appreciation of the ability and willingness of middle-level and even lower-level organization members to coordinate activities across departmental lines and (2) a recognition that upper management's job appropriately entailed creating decision-making mechanisms, routes for information transfer, and criteria for performance rather than the actual making of resource-allocation decisions.

THE LOGIC OF EACH ORGANIZATIONAL FORM

Simply describing and illustrating common organizational forms, as we have done, is only a start in achieving corporate success. The term "form" suggests not only an *internal arrangement* of resources but an *external orientation* as well. Moreover, the concept of form implies an *operating logic* that governs both internal and external processes when the form is put into use. An organization's form, in this sense, is an arrangement of resources ready to receive and act on a set of inputs in a predictable sequence of steps. Lastly, an organizational form not only arranges resources and directs their actions, it also *teaches*—that is, it provides a practical rationale for collective action, clarifying the contributions of each unit and explaining how it relates to others in the organization. The core characteristics of each of the organizational forms discussed so far are shown in Table 2-2.

Table 2–2
OPERATING LOGIC OF
TRADITIONAL ORGANIZATIONAL FORMS

Form	Core Operating Logic
Functional	Focusing a special-purpose machine. Creating cost efficient production of standard goods or services through the centrally planned and controlled activities of departments of functional specialists.
Divisional	Creating centrally aimed and financed islands of autonomy. Product and/or service innovation created through autonomous divisional operating decisions coupled with corporate responsibility for strategic investments and resource allocation.
Matrix	Creating a complicated, delicate balance through a focus on both *efficiency* (needs of functional departments or global product divisions) and local *responsiveness* (needs of project teams or regional markets) achieved through lateral coordination.

THE FUNCTIONAL FORM: A SPECIAL-PURPOSE MACHINE

The functional organization, employed today by many if not most Defender firms, can be thought of as a special-purpose machine designed to produce a limited line of goods or services in large volume and at low cost. Hence the logic of the functional organization is *centrally coordinated specialization*. Departments, each staffed with technical experts in numbers established by a central budget, repeatedly make their contribution to the firm's overall effort in accordance with a common schedule. To be successful, the functional organization's specialized skills and equipment must be fully and predictably utilized. A functionally structured manufacturing firm, for example, can efficiently produce a limited array of products if demand for those products can be forecast and production runs strictly scheduled. However, if the number of products offered becomes too large, or if demand variations interfere with efficient scheduling, the functional organization begins to prove inflexible and costly to operate.

Over time, well-designed functional organizations increase their capabilities through further growth in specialized skills and continued improvement in coordination and problem-solving routines. This increased capacity is available for penetration into existing and closely related markets, which is the strategy employed by Defender firms. Managers in such organizations develop a sort of tunnel vision. They witness their companies serving the same or similar markets, and they see investments being made in specialized operating systems. In effect, they learn how to do things better rather than how to do new or different things.

THE DIVISIONAL FORM: ISLANDS OF AUTONOMY

The divisional organization, frequently used by Prospector firms, can be thought of as a collection of similar special-purpose machines, each independently operated to serve a particular market and centrally evaluated on the basis of economic performance for possible expansion, contraction, or redirection. As envisioned in the 1920s by Alfred Sloan at General Motors, by Robert Wood at Sears, Roebuck, and later by Ralph Cordiner at General Electric, and others, the logic of the divisional organization is the *coupling of divisional autonomy with centrally controlled performance evaluation and resource allocation.* The divisional form offers the flexibility necessary to develop product-line breadth through its ability to focus resources rapidly on new or expanding markets. It also allows for the development of mechanisms for transferring new technology and managerial know-how across divisions as well as into newly created or acquired operations. Overall, the divisional organization's ability to reallocate management know-how and emerging technology, along with resources generated from existing operations, gives it an advantage in responding to new opportunities and fronting the cost of start-up—exactly the capabilities required by the Prospector strategy.

In order for the divisional organization to work effectively, corporate management must refrain from engaging in operating decisions more appropriately made at the divisional level. Instead, its role is to plan divisional goals with division managers and then evaluate divisional performance at the end of the operating period. Division managers who work in this milieu learn to be independent and entrepreneurial. Not only do they try to expand their division's existing business, they also search for new areas of growth outside their current domain. Thus, in the aggregate, managers in the divisional organization are continually pushing it further and further afield.

THE MATRIX FORM:
A COMPLICATED AND DELICATE BALANCE

The matrix organization, often visible in Analyzer firms, can be thought of as a complex machine simultaneously generating two or more outputs for a set of both stable and changing markets. The operating logic of the stable portion of the matrix form is similar to that of the functional form, that is, centrally coordinated specialization. Not surprisingly, the portion responding to unique or changeable markets emphasizes local operating autonomy, as is the case in the divisional form. To these dual aspects of its operating logic, the matrix organization adds the requirement for *balance among the components, to produce mutually beneficial allocations of resources.* Matrix organizations work best when the proportion of the company's total resources focused on temporary or customized projects is significantly smaller than the proportion focused on more stable, long-term projects. Otherwise, with so many resources in flux, the organization's resource-allocation mechanisms simply become overloaded.

Matrix managers have complex jobs, and what they are "taught" by matrix structures and processes can be similarly complex and sophisticated. For example, most matrix managers must learn how to function effectively without formal authority. Also, they have to learn how to communicate with a variety of people from different technical specialties. On the project side of a matrix organization, because managers spend a considerable amount of time working with customers, consultants, and others outside the organization, they learn how the company's resources are connected to the market. Moreover, because some functional specialists are regularly rotated into project manager positions, an expanding group of matrix managers learns how to become business generalists.

IDEOLOGICAL REQUIREMENTS

To this point, we have seen how leading-edge firms respond to new environmental demands by inventing new strategies and developing the structures and processes required to make them work. Such new organizational forms work best when managers have a wide and deep understanding of the operating logic that guides the use of the form. However, even with an organizational form and its operating logic in place, one essential element for the successful functioning of a company is missing. That element is managerial ideology—a value system that defines and explains how people should be managed in the new form. Unless a new organizational form is supported and energized by an appropriate managerial ideology, its competitive advantages will never be fully realized.

In each of the historical periods described above, managers in the pioneering firms did not create entirely new management philosophies.[8] They assimilated and pieced together ideas and changes that were occurring in the broader society. For example, before the functional organization could replace the small owner-managed firms of the time, managers had to move away from the traditional philosophy of management, in which employees were essentially viewed as hired hands who worked only for money, to a *human relations philosophy* that acknowledged management's responsibility in enabling employee success (see Table 2–3). This new view of employees emphasized the humanity of even the lowest-level workers, stressing their eagerness to respond to managerial praise and attention. The progressive managers of the time recognized the importance of a stable, loyal work force to the ultimate success of the functional form. They managed employees in a way that ensured the needed work-force continuity.

Table 2–3
THEORIES OF MANAGEMENT

Traditional model	Human Relations model	Human Resources model
Assumptions:	*Assumptions:*	*Assumptions:*
1. Work is inherently distasteful to most people	1. People want to feel useful and important	1. Work is not inherently distasteful. People want to contribute to meaningful goals which they have helped establish
2. What workers do is less important than what they earn for doing it	2. People desire to belong and to be recognized as individuals	
3. Few want or can handle work which requires creativity, self-direction, or self-control	3. These needs are more important than money in motivating people to work	2. Most people can exercise far more creative, responsible self-direction and self-control than their present jobs demand
Policies:	*Policies:*	*Policies:*
1. The manager's basic task is to closely supervise and control subordinates	1. The manager's basic task is to make each worker feel useful and important	1. The manager's basic task is to make use of "untapped" human resources
2. The manager must break tasks down into simple, repetitive, easily learned operations	2. The manager should keep subordinates informed and listen to their objections to plans	2. The manager must create an environment in which all members may contribute to the limits of their ability
3. The manager must establish detailed work routines and procedures and enforce these firmly but fairly	3. The manager should allow subordinates to exercise some self-control on routine matters	3. The manager must encourage full participation on important matters, continually broadening subordinate self-direction and control
Expectations:	*Expectations:*	*Expectations:*
1. People can tolerate work if the pay is decent and the boss is fair	1. Sharing information with subordinates and involving them in routine decisions will satisfy their basic needs to belong and to feel important	1. Expanding subordinate influence, self-direction, and self-control will lead to direct improvements in operating efficiency
2. If tasks are simple enough and people are closely controlled, they will produce up to standard	2. Satisfying these needs will improve morale and reduce resistance to formal authority—subordinates will "willingly cooperate"	2. Work satisfaction may improve as a "by-product" of subordinates making full use of their resources

Source: Raymond E. Miles, *Theories of Management*, McGraw-Hill, New York 1975, Figure 3–1. Reproduced with permission of McGraw-Hill.

This same philosophy, however, was not able to meet the challenge of managing people in the divisional organization. The divisional form demanded more than paternalistic management; it required tapping into a broad range of employee knowledge and skills. Again, the pioneers of the divisional organization, such as General Motors, had a much easier time articulating a new managerial ideology than did their peers. The new *human resources philosophy,* which assumed that managers and employees wanted to use their full capabilities in the service of the organization, matched up nicely with the decentralized processes associated with the divisional form. Company managements that adopted, or already possessed, this philosophy found it less difficult to implement the divisional structure.

When the matrix form arrived, it called for even greater use of the human resources philosophy—both in substance and in application to lower organizational levels. Unfortunately, few managers in early matrix organizations had moved much beyond the human relations philosophy, so the complex demands of the matrix structure constantly ran into ideological barriers. And, as matrix organizations increasingly began to suffer operating problems in the 1970s and early 1980s, many managers reverted to traditional ideological views, questioning the logic of the matrix form as well as the competence of their subordinates. In actuality, however, it was their own beliefs and attitudes that doomed early matrix structures to failure or prevented the development of mechanisms to speed up the decision-making process in more advanced matrix organizations.

CONCLUSION

During periods of transition, a few firms achieve early tight fit by pioneering a new organizational form. Most firms, however, achieve only minimal fit—and many of these hover near conditions of misfit. Historically, the largest barrier to success for these companies has been the slow adoption of a managerial ideology that fits the desired organizational form. We are in such a transition period at the moment, as the next chapter describes.

CHAPTER 3

THE MODERN
TRANSITION

In each of the three historical periods described in Chapter 2, a new organizational form was developed that built upon the previous one. The general prescription for success in each period was thought to be the same: "Get bigger and stronger." Specifically, diversified firms in the 1950s grew to vast size by reproducing for each new market or geographic region a division that largely replicated the special-purpose functional organization of the earlier period. Similarly, the multiproduct, multinational matrix organizations of the 1970s used combinations of the functional and divisional forms to create economic machines of enormous strength and complexity.

However, in sharp contrast to the transitions associated with these earlier periods, which were marked by creative organizational improvements and extensions, the current transition is a revolution, one that has its roots in the 1970s but has intensified in the last decade. For most firms during this transitional period, the older prescriptions of growth, integration, and operating synergy have proven increasingly unproductive. In fact, many of the key organizational assets of earlier periods, such as corporate planning and coordination mechanisms, appear now to be liabilities.

In this chapter, we will first briefly recount the characteristics of the current transition—the forces shaping the revolution. Next, we will describe three models of success visible in a variety of today's leading firms. One model, illustrated by the cases of Wal-Mart and Rubbermaid, is the modern application of an older organizational form. A second model, represented by the experiences of Chrysler Corporation, Harley-Davidson, and General Electric, involves the total redesign of the firm's strategy, structure, and process. The third model is presently evolving from the search by numerous firms for a new—or at least improved—recipe for success, one that is often referred to as the "network organization." Finally, after discussing these specific models of success, we will explain why the majority of today's firms are finding the attainment of success during the transitional period so difficult.

TODAY'S COMPETITIVE ENVIRONMENT: CAUSES AND EFFECTS

The key factors underlying the current revolution are globalization and technological change. These forces are interacting to produce an accelerated pace of technology transfer from one industry to another and from one global marketplace to another. Moreover, in virtually every industrialized country, a trend toward deregulation and the privatization of government-owned enterprises is contributing to technological diffusion and increased competition.

Globalization, viewed for many years by U.S. firms as a spectre, is today an accepted reality. At least 70 to 85 percent of the U.S. economy is now in direct contact with, and usually feeling pressure from, foreign competition. In growing strength and numbers, foreign competitors reduce profit margins on low-end goods to the barest minimum, and they innovate across high-end products at ever-increasing rates. Further, the key to the success of foreign competitors is not only lower wage levels, fewer environmental regulations, or government investment policies. Instead, the strength of foreign competition is increasingly built on heavy investment in capital equipment, extensive training in new techniques and technologies, and large research and development expenditures.

These latter characteristics help explain the driving force of technological change. The United States, once the world's leader in new product and process design, frequently finds itself trailing in both areas today. Whether measured by the number of patents issued, the number of computer-controlled processes employed, or the proportion of Americans earning scientific and technical degrees, the U.S. leadership position is either threatened or has been surpassed in industry after industry. Thus, with more and more competitors able to make and exploit technological changes, the pace of change inevitably quickens, product life cycles are invariably shortened, and adaptive sophistication and speed are increasingly a firm's key assets.

As technologically sophisticated products and services proliferate around the world, even emerging economies can assimilate the new knowledge and begin to invest in training and physical assets. The time required for technological gains to transfer from the most advanced economies to those in the newly industrialized ranks and eventually to those in the emerging stages of industrialization is becoming ever shorter. Firms thus find it difficult to build insulating barriers of either technology or location around their businesses.

Given the magnitude and intensity of these environmental changes, the uncertainty and confusion felt by managers in many U.S. firms are hardly surprising. The constant discovery of new competitors, the shrinking of profit margins, and the demand for increased quality and service place stresses on firms that their existing packages of strategy, structure, and process were not designed to handle. It is clear that many of the assets that firms accumulated during the growth years are now underemployed and costly compared to the value they add to a company's output. The phrase "spending more and earning less" is unfortunately becoming increasingly applicable to many companies.

Similarly, it is clear that no matter how hard many firms work to make their organizations respond to the rapid changes occurring in the marketplace, they always appear to be behind. Companies have found again and again that the minimal time it takes, with no mistakes or resistance, to plan and execute a major design change is considerably longer than the life cycle of new products emerging in their industries.

To meet these challenges, managers have been offered a wide array of prescriptions. They are urged to downsize, get rid of underutilized assets, and cut back on the number of layers of underemployed middle managers—prescriptions that many firms have administered with a vengeance. The typical Fortune 1000 firm is considerably smaller today than a decade ago, with over two million middle-management positions eliminated. Nevertheless, many firms have discovered that downsizing alone is not enough—they have merely gone from being large dysfunctional organizations to being smaller ones.

Firms have also been urged to reduce their degree of vertical integration, to focus on that point along the value chain where they have the competence to add the greatest value, and to outsource the remaining activities. Following this prescription, the global search for inexpensive and efficient outsourcing partners has accelerated rapidly over the past decade, bringing new plants and offices into being across a growing group of newly industrialized economies. However, for many firms, the rush to outsourcing has not proven to be the solution to all of their problems. Countries with low-cost labor and materials markets become higher-cost economies as firms compete for their resources, and a low-cost supplier available to one firm is inevitably matched or superceded by one located elsewhere.

In addition to cost cutting and speed of adaptation, managers are reminded that the new global requirement is total quality assurance. However, for many managers, the demand for quality responsibility adds to concerns about loss of operating control through the reduction of technical staff and outsourcing. Overall, the current transition is fraught with far more challenges than opportunities, and there is far less evidence of accomplishment than examples of failure. Companies currently enjoying success are, therefore, worth examining in detail.

WAL-MART AND RUBBERMAID: NEW VERSIONS OF TRADITIONAL ORGANIZATIONAL FORMS

Two companies currently enjoying recognition and success are Wal-Mart and Rubbermaid. Both have achieved tight internal and external fit in their respective packages of strategy, structure, and process by intelligently adapting time-tested organizational ingredients to meet the demands of the current environment.

WAL-MART: MACHINE-LIKE EFFICIENCY WITH A HUMAN TOUCH[1]

Founded prior to the current period but largely a phenomenon of the 1980s, Wal-Mart is an example of a functional organization, obeying the operating logic pioneered by Carnegie Steel and other turn-of-the-century firms, but modified to deal with the requirements of the modern marketplace. Functionally structured firms were originally created to supply voracious, expanding national markets with standardized goods and services at reasonable prices. Hungry for goods they could afford, consumers of the day were willing to accept constraints on the size, color, and number of models that companies offered in order to gain cost efficiencies. For example, by producing one model in one color, Ford Motor Company was able to offer the nation the first affordable car for the masses.

However, while large markets for efficiently produced standardized goods were becoming increasingly common at the turn of the century, today's complex and sophisticated markets demand careful segmentation if companies are to succeed with a limited-line, limited-size, cost-based approach. A major portion of Wal-Mart's strategic excellence can be attributed to its ability to limit its expansion efforts to retail locations with similar geographic and demographic characteristics. Virtually all of Wal-Mart's over two thousand stores are located in small towns or suburbs of medium-size cities, are built for transportation and parking ease, and are staffed with well-trained personnel from low to moderately priced labor markets.

In effect, by carefully locating its stores in homogeneous settings, Wal-Mart has made a complex national market more simple and predictable. Having stabilized its market, Wal-Mart makes maximum use of computerized, on-line sales data to feed what is widely recognized as one of the most efficient inventory and distribution systems in the country. Like its functional predecessors, Wal-Mart performs a limited set of functions extremely well, using the specialized talents of planners and logistics specialists equipped with the most modern and sophisticated equipment. These specialists provide a flow of on-time, ready-to-shelve goods to well-trained and informed store personnel who are imbued with the Wal-Mart culture of helpful, friendly service. On a day-to-day basis, much of the Wal-Mart system operates like a huge vending machine, gathering data for replenishment needs in real time as goods pass through the checkout lines. It is, in other words, an electronically based management by exception system, demanding direct management attention only when unusual events occur.

Although Wal-Mart has from its inception professed a strong commitment to developing and utilizing its human resources, a philosophy that tends to be associated with more recently developed organizational forms, it makes no apology for making key operating decisions centrally. To the extent that merchandising decisions can be made centrally, even if store inventories are managed regionally, Wal-Mart can provide suppliers with attractive orders that, even with low margins, can be profitably planned in advance and delivered just in time. Managers and employees throughout the organization are encouraged by philosophy, culture, and rewards to make suggestions for improvement, but the key decisions are appropriately and efficiently centralized.

Is Wal-Mart thus a model for all firms to follow in this transitional period? Clearly not. It is a model only for those firms that are prepared to limit their growth to markets whose homogeneity allows them to utilize their unique ability to deliver standardized goods or services with excellent quality-to-cost ratios. Moreover, the Wal-Mart operating logic only works if firms are prepared to maintain high levels of investment in specialized personnel and equipment to guarantee the continuation of their cost advantage, and only if they are prepared to put some of the monetary gains of their efficiency efforts into improved customer service (e.g., by employing greeters or giving bonuses to employees).

RUBBERMAID: DIVISIONALIZING INNOVATION[2]

Another of today's corporate success stories is Rubbermaid. This company, like Wal-Mart, was born prior to the current period but has enjoyed its greatest success and recognition only in the last several years. Also like Wal-Mart, Rubbermaid is an example of an earlier organizational form applied with creativity and vision to a complex and demanding modern marketplace.

Unlike Wal-Mart, however, the secret of Rubbermaid's success is not the development of state-of-the-art, centralized planning, inventory, and distribution systems. To the contrary, Rubbermaid has succeeded by decentralizing key product design decisions to its various operating divisions. Over three hundred new products per year flow from the autonomous research and development units located in each division and focused exclusively on that division's product market. Rubbermaid's new products are not the result of finding new ways to mold plastic. Instead, they represent both substantive and stylistic product innovations that can be brought to market with existing manufacturing technologies. As such, these products reflect Rubbermaid's image of innovation and high quality—an image that has built strong customer loyalty and a wide retail shelf-space advantage for Rubbermaid over its lower-cost competitors.

For Wal-Mart, predictability is a major asset. For Rubbermaid, it is a threat. Indeed, Rubbermaid views change as an opportunity and defines its role as that of constantly creating the changes and improvements that drive its markets. Rubbermaid is so confident of its product design competence, and so protective of the fruits of its own creativity, that it seldom engages in traditional forms of test marketing. This is because Rubbermaid's managers and research personnel have invested so thoroughly in understanding their segmented markets. Rubbermaid merely makes what its customers want and puts the product on the market.

Rubbermaid's divisions, however, are not completely autonomous. Because many of the products from different divisions are distributed through the same retail outlets, some marketing and most sales activities are organized along common distribution channels. Nevertheless, the key resources necessary for rapid adaptation to the needs of Rubbermaid's several product lines are housed at the divisional level. Design decisions made locally, unencumbered by lengthy review processes, guarantee an edge in innovation and allow the corporate office to manage by objectives, rewarding divisions for meeting the goal of increased sales for both existing and new products.

If Wal-Mart is not the new organizational model to emulate, is it Rubbermaid? Again, the answer is no. Rubbermaid is a model for those firms that face, or believe they can develop, markets for related but diversified goods or services with unique features. The model only works for firms that, like Rubbermaid, are willing to truly decentralize key operating decisions to the divisional level in order to achieve rapid and distinctive responsiveness. A corporate group not prepared to limit its operating role to leaving the divisions alone except for joint goal-setting and market boundary determinations will not obtain the benefits of divisionalization enjoyed by Rubbermaid. In fact, a corporate management that goes beyond these limits bears the costs of decentralization without obtaining its benefits—it pays for divisional expertise but then does not employ it. Instead, Rubbermaid illustrates an organizational model that can be used under similar market circumstances by corporate managers who understand its logic and invest their own talents by creating new divisions and by financing the expansion of existing divisions that are enjoying major success.

REDESIGNING COMPANIES IN TROUBLE

In the space of a few months at the end of 1992 and the beginning of 1993, the CEOs of General Motors, IBM, Westinghouse Electric, and American Express were ousted, and Sears, Roebuck and several other companies were under heavy fire. The pressures brought about by large shifts in markets and technology, as well as by the growth of foreign and domestic competition, were magnified by the continuing impact of a global recession. As a result of these pressures, earnings crumbled into losses. The strategic and structural frailty of firms that had long been viewed as the invincible champions of American industry was brought clearly into focus.

In fact, the corporate bloodletting of the winter of 1993 was simply a particularly dramatic moment in a multiyear drama that is still going on. For many leading U.S. firms, the struggle to find new ways to meet the demands of the global marketplace has proved to be a multiact tragedy with no happy ending in sight.

For a handful of firms, however, major efforts at total redesign have been undertaken successfully, some temporarily and others for longer periods of time. The redesign efforts at three such companies—Chrysler Corporation, Harley-Davidson, and General Electric—are notable for different reasons.

CHRYSLER CORPORATION AND HARLEY-DAVIDSON: CUTTING BACK TO ACHIEVE SUCCESS[3]

The widely publicized turnarounds at Chrysler and Harley-Davidson share several characteristics. Each company accumulated weaknesses over the years, and each was essentially nursed back to health with government aid—Chrysler's in the form of a direct financial bailout and Harley-Davidson by the imposition of quotas and tariffs on foreign competitors' products.

Chrysler and Harley-Davidson found success by redesigning

both strategy and structure, creating a new package with a much clearer logic. At Chrysler, customers were reattracted by new automotive designs: convertibles, minivans, and totally reshaped models of several passenger cars. However, these changes alone would not have saved the firm. Changes had to be made—in fact, could only be made—in conjunction with a total redesign of organizational structure and management processes. The crucial initial steps at Chrysler included dramatic cutbacks in the number of models designed and produced, focusing the attention of the product and process design departments on a limited line for which significant styling innovations and quality improvements could be achieved. To round out its product line, Chrysler turned to foreign manufacturers who supplied certain types of vehicles. In effect, the Chrysler redesign brought its strategy back into line with its structure, a centralized design and production organization that was always competent but had been stretched beyond its limits.

Similarly, Harley-Davidson, under a temporary reprieve provided by government intervention, revamped both its strategy and its structure, which in the company's estimation had to be made together. Harley's market strategy was to convince a broader public that its models matched or exceeded both the design features and quality of its foreign competitors. Harley could only deliver on these claims, however, by redesigning its entire internal structure as well as its dealer and marketing systems.

At Chrysler, the breadth of the product line was reduced to meet styling and production abilities. At Harley, the length of the value chain managed by the company was reduced by outsourcing many component parts and supplies, which allowed Harley managers and employees to focus their efforts on improving quality and reducing manufacturing and inventory waste. With improved product design and quality to raise customer interest and expectations, dealers were strongly encouraged to improve customer service, attraction, and retention. Thus, as at Chrysler, Harley-Davidson's effort was one of total redesign.

GENERAL ELECTRIC: A REDESIGN PIONEER[4]

While the redesign experiences at Chrysler and Harley-Davidson are both impressive and instructive, perhaps the most intriguing success story of the last decade is that of General Electric. GE's experience is valuable because, almost alone among the former giants of U.S. industry, it has come through the vortex of the last decade and emerged with a clarity of vision and operating logic that appear well-suited and strong enough to carry the company successfully into the next period. It is valuable also because GE has produced a total package of strategy, structure, and process that not only exhibits a high degree of fit but also includes the managerial ideology required to maintain that fit over time. Finally, GE's story is worth telling because it demonstrates that it is possible for a firm to identify growing problems in a timely fashion, to take action before its resources are depleted, and to carry the redesign process to its logical conclusion even after major successes have been achieved.

In its early stages, GE's redesign efforts followed the same script played out today in virtually every large U.S. firm. Typically, a slowdown in earnings growth, coupled with increasing pressure from adept domestic and foreign competitors, created concern about the company's future viability. GE, too, questioned the prospects of many of its businesses as it headed into the decade of the 1980s. However, unlike most of its peers, GE moved quickly to launch a dramatic downsizing and cost-cutting program heavily focused on corporate overhead, particularly the elimination of financial planners and other staff specialists. In the 1950s, GE had been, along with General Motors and Sears, Roebuck, one of the pillars of the community of firms following a strategy of related diversification by structuring themselves into divisions and decentralizing operating control. During the 1960s and 1970s, GE built a huge corporate staff in the pursuit of increased research, operating, and financial synergy. GE's version of then-popular "portfolio" models to guide corporate strategic decision making was widely lauded and imitated.

Round after round of downsizing and cost cutting were carried out in the mid-1980s, with a speed and human cost that brought GE's chairman, Jack Welch, both praise and enmity from a variety of quarters. Welch publicly recognized the human costs of the cuts and their continuing effect on morale with a major effort to restore purpose and commitment among GE's remaining managers and employees. In 1988, he began to refer to the way the company worked as the "GE growth engine." In the ensuing months and years, he made numerous presentations to clarify and explain the logic of the "new" GE. Essentially, this logic included:

- Corporate strategy—Focus only on businesses where the company has the ability to add significant value. Become number one or number two in each of those businesses.
- Divisional structure—Present division managers with a clear challenge (become number one or number two) and restore operational autonomy. Allocate human and financial resources to divisions where the growth is. Measure performance by earnings contributed to the company through market growth, volume, and productivity improvement.
- Financial system—Use cash generated by the divisions to pay dividends and make acquisitions, and then return excess cash to the divisions for further investment.
- Management philosophy—Manage all employees of the company according to a philosophy whose core values are *speed* (achieved by freeing division managers and employees from corporate controls); *simplicity* (achieved through a program called "Work-out," in which leaders and their teams figure out how to simplify and quicken the process of their business); and *self-confidence* (achieved by creating an environment in which all employees in the company can see and feel a connection between what they do and winning in the marketplace).

General Electric's successful efforts at a total redesign are notable in that they were begun before downsizing and cost cutting became a standard operating procedure in American business. More important, however, GE took action before it was in desperate shape. This bought the company the time that it needed to redefine its organizational package and make the necessary changes. Finally, and perhaps most critical to GE's current success, management was able to articulate a clear logic for operating the company and to support that logic with a human resource management approach that promised to continue to build appropriate competencies throughout the organization.

AN EMERGING ORGANIZATIONAL FORM

Alongside success stories such as Wal-Mart and Rubbermaid, which have made innovative use of older organizational forms, and General Electric, which has survived the process of total redesign, a third scenario of success is emerging. In this scenario, firms achieve success through the use of a new organizational form—a new way of packaging strategy, structure, and process. However, this new form is very much a work in progress, one for which the operating logic and the supporting managerial ideology are as yet only partially articulated and understood.

The new form eschews the traditional ingredients of corporate success such as "do everything yourself." It does not call for complete vertical integration or tall management hierarchies. Instead, the newest form of organization relies on ingredients such as value-chain location based on core competencies, strategic alliances, outsourcing, and, wherever possible, the substitution of market forces for hierarchical controls. This new form is called the "network organization."

Network organizations can be found in newer industries where technological change occurs so rapidly that firms can concentrate effectively only on a limited segment of the total value chain. The leading firms in the biotechnology industry, for example, primarily resemble large research and development departments as opposed to the vertically integrated pharmaceutical firms that design, produce, and market chemically based medicines. Similarly, in the computer industry, the limited focus of companies such as Dell Computer (assembly and distribution) and Intel (chip design and manufacturing) allows goods and services to flow to the marketplace through a constantly changing network of companies and relationships.

The network form of organization can also be found in mature industries where large companies have disaggregated to cut costs and increase responsiveness. For example, although U.S. automobile manufacturers have reduced the proportion of total value added by their own production by as much as 10 to 15 percent in the last ten years, they still have not become as adept at developing and utilizing mutually beneficial just-in-time delivery relationships with their suppliers as their Japanese and some of their European competitors.

Last, inside many companies there are the beginnings of what Russell Ackoff has called "corporate perestroika," the substitution of internal market mechanisms for centrally planned administrative mechanisms.[5] That is, instead of attempting to control the flow of goods and services between internal corporate units using administrative mechanisms such as plans, schedules, and transfer prices, units are permitted to buy and sell goods and services at market prices—including going outside the company if internal units cannot match external price or quality. Increasingly, corporate staff groups, including transportation services, training and development, and even strategic planning, now sell their services to operating divisions and to outside clients as well. For example, Workforce Solutions, IBM's former corporate human resource group, sells its services to IBM business units and other companies, placing it in direct competition with consulting firms that offer similar services.

We have categorized these and hundreds of other examples into three generic network forms: dynamic, stable, and internal (see Figure 3–1).[6]

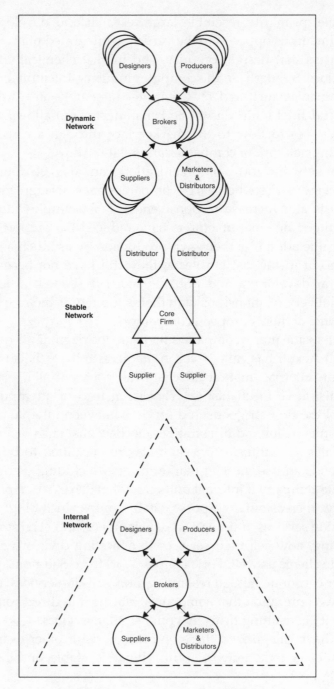

Figure 3–1   Common Network Types

DYNAMIC NETWORKS

In general, dynamic networks emerge in settings where rapid technological advances, faddish shifts in customer tastes, or short time horizons make response time a critical factor in success and make investments in costly, special-purpose assets risky. In these situations, firms want to hold only those assets that they can employ fully and flexibly. This means that a given firm is likely to focus on a portion of the value chain and to forge relationships with other specialist firms to offer the final product or service. Lewis Galoob Toys, for example, relies on independent inventors and entertainment companies to conceive its products, while outside specialists do most of the design and engineering. Galoob contracts for manufacturing and packaging with a dozen or so vendors in Hong Kong, and they in turn pass on the most labor-intensive work to factories in China. When the toys arrive in the United States, Galoob distributes through commissioned manufacturers' representatives. Galoob does not even collect its accounts. It sells its receivables to a factoring company that also sets Galoob's credit policy. In short, Galoob is the chief broker among all these independent specialist firms.

STABLE NETWORKS

Stable networks tend to appear in mature industries with somewhat predictable market cycles and demands. More often than not, stable networks form around a few large, key firms for which network partners provide either upstream services, such as the supply of parts and components, or downstream services such as distribution. These clusters of firms interact more regularly than those in the dynamic network. Because their relationships are more limited and predictable, stable network partners develop standardized interaction routines. In Japan, these relationships usually include some element of shared ownership as part of an all-encompassing *keiretsu*.[7] In the United States, ties are usually not as familial, but long-lasting stable network relationships are commonplace. For example, in the athletic footwear and apparel business, Nike has had long-established relationships with a broad network of suppliers and distributors around the world.

INTERNAL NETWORKS

Internal networks emerge inside large organizations as resource flows become increasingly unpredictable or costly. In large universities, for example, new teaching and research programs are begun by offering directorships to interested faculty along with funds to compensate the departments for the time of members or other colleagues who wish to work part-time or temporarily in the new programs. If the new programs ultimately prove to be stable areas of research and teaching, formal departments may be created. This approach, a market-driven matrix, has been approximated in many firms over the last decade and is beginning to blossom into total internal networks in some large multinational companies. For example, the global electrical products firm ABB Asea Brown Boveri buys and sells goods across company and country boundaries at market prices, which permits performance evaluation of all its myriad business units on the basis of actual profitability.

MISSING INGREDIENTS IN THE NEW FORM

Even though there is widespread recognition of the network organizational form and a growing number of firms have attempted to use it, many if not most of these applications are occurring without all of the essential ingredients in place. For many firms, the operating logic of the network organization— what it is, what it is intended to do, and what its costs, benefits, and limitations are—is only partially internalized.

For example, many firms have turned to the network form of organization because they felt forced to do so. They discovered, perhaps, that they can no longer meet competitors' prices by operating their own facilities, and therefore they join in the search for low-cost suppliers or distributors. Such firms enter their network relationships defensively and without having clearly thought through the nature of the relationships they are attempting to build with their network partners. In these situations, firms may attempt either to exploit their upstream or downstream partners or to protect themselves from possible problems by burdening their relationships with costly contractual procedures.

In the long run, as we will discuss in Part 4, network relationships driven only by cost-savings goals will not be productive. Recall that the functional, divisional, and matrix organizations emerged to allow firms to respond to the opportunities posed by new market environments. They required extensive investments in new technical and managerial know-how in order to perform at levels far exceeding the capacity of earlier organizational forms. Firms attempting to use the network form solely as a cost-saving substitute for some aspects of their current operation are not internalizing a complete network logic. A complete logic calls for all network elements to be investment-based—to be chosen to operate at a given point along the value chain not because of a temporary cost advantage due to low wages or minimal environmental regulations, but because of a unique people- or equipment-based competence.

In addition, few managers have as yet explored and articulated the fit between the network form and their own philosophies of management—their views about people and how they can and should be managed. Both externally across units in the network and internally within the manager's own unit, the network form demands attitudes and behaviors that are not part of many managers' experience. For example, managers conditioned to exercising hierarchical control over all the elements needed for the production of goods or services may well be uncomfortable dealing with an independent supplier. Or, managers used to appealing to their superiors for additional time or resources may find it difficult to adapt to the discipline of the marketplace. Last, in order to meet the rapid response times required in the most dynamic networks, each unit must utilize its own resources fully and with great flexibility—a speed- and change-oriented approach that is outside the experience of many of today's managers.

CONCLUSION

In this chapter, two key points have been closely interwoven. First, it should be clear from the company examples cited that even in this difficult period of transition some firms are succeeding—some by applying old organizational forms innovatively, others by recognizing early the shortcomings that prompted total redesign, and a growing number by experimenting with a new form created to respond to new technological and market conditions. Second, while some companies are succeeding, most are not realizing the potential of their resources. For this larger group, the current period continues to be one of frustration and disappointment. Moreover, most of these firms, in their own minds at least, have tried all the things that the successful companies have done but with little or no success. In fact, in the front ranks of this group are some failed experimenters with the network form, firms that wrote off the new organizational approach even before it was fully developed.

To understand this particular group of companies and, in the process, to clarify the meaning of fit, we must next explore the dynamics of failure. In fact, for many of the firms in the failure group, an understanding not only of why they are failing but of how they became failures is absolutely essential to their subsequent renewal and success.

PART TWO

WHY ORGANIZATIONS FAIL

No organization wants or needs a recipe for failure. What organizations do need, however, is a thorough understanding of organizational pathology. Just as a medical doctor needs an understanding of the parts, connections, and flows of the human body—and where and how these are likely to fail—managers need a grasp of how, where, and why organizational linkages, resource allocations, and coordination mechanisms can and frequently do go awry.

Of course, like human systems, organizations can fail for no reason of their own. Just as a hiker may be struck by lightning or a pedestrian hit by a truck, an organization can be blind-sided by such occurrences as a sudden change in regulatory policy or a stock market downturn while it's in the midst of going public. Nevertheless, as is the case with humans, the etiology of most organizational maladies includes some preventable causes.

In Chapter 4, we will discuss organizational failure and its major causes, identifying two generic types of failure. Both types of failure have occurred as a result of managerial decisions in every period as well as across all forms of organization. We will show how these two major dysfunctions are part of a broader framework of failure dynamics—an unfolding, incremental process of decline. In Chapter 5, we discuss the first type of organizational failure: a delayed or inappropriate response to changes in the environment. In Chapter 6, we describe a more intriguing and insidious type of failure that occurs when managers unknowingly undo the organizational fit within their own companies.

CHAPTER 4

THE PROCESS OF MISFIT

In order to achieve the purpose of this book—helping managers understand and construct strategy, structure, and process fit—an awareness of how and why misfit occurs and persists is essential. In fact, here we shift the focus entirely from fit to misfit. Describing misfit and failure, particularly from a post-mortem perspective, is frequently more dramatic. Moreover, predicting organizational failure is easier than predicting success, which is a little like forecasting individual human longevity. That is, a doctor cannot guarantee that recipes for good health will produce an octogenarian. However, medical science can easily be used to show someone how to increase his or her odds of an early death.

It is our intent to avoid the temptation to be polemical. Managers gain little and may lose a lot from a preoccupation with organizational failure. Just as in sports, a positive image of achievement is important—a team that plays to win is usually more successful than one that plays to avoid defeat. Nevertheless, to continue with a sports analogy, even though a baseball player needs to go to the plate with a clear and positive mental image of his or her batting stroke, the hitting instructor and the player may wish to review videotapes of the player's swing if batting average begins to slip.

When athletes in a slump view pictures of their performance, they often see common mistakes that should have been avoided but were not. Recognizing these mistakes and refocusing on a plan of positive achievement are both needed. Recognizing correctable mistakes early helps avoid their becoming deeply ingrained in the athlete's routines. But success still depends on doing the right things well, not just avoiding the wrong things. It is from this perspective that we examine organizational misfit and failure.

GENERIC TYPES OF ORGANIZATIONAL FAILURE

Occasional situations of misfit and failure are beyond managerial anticipation and/or influence. Just as airline passengers can do little more than carry insurance against the rare catastrophe, managers cannot foresee or prevent some forms of organizational failure. Of course, some "natural disasters" can sometimes be anticipated—for example, a delay in regulatory approval of a start-up biotech firm's first product—but for our purposes, we will exclude such possible misjudgments and misfortunes from our analysis. Instead, we will focus on those types of failure that result directly from faulty managerial decisions and behaviors (see Table 4–1).

Two generic types of managerially induced misfit and failure are easily described, though difficult to avoid. The first of these are failures resulting from not responding quickly or appropriately to environmental changes—changes that were visible or easily forecastable and for which other firms in similar settings were able to make successful adjustments. For example, in the transition from one major period to the next, Hall of Fame companies move quickly to recognize and adapt to changes in the technological, social, and market environment. Tight-fit firms may not enjoy first-mover success, but they move quickly and completely to achieve excellent performance. Minimal-fit firms, however, move too slowly or only partially to take advantage of the opportunities available in the new period. These firms, as noted earlier, do not fail, but their marginal success does them or society little good—the assets they utilize are never fully employed, and both human and capital resources are wasted. Finally, misfit firms move so slowly, so minimally, or so ineptly that failure is the inevitable result. In fact, some misfit firms

Table 4–1
MAJOR FORMS OF MISFIT

Externally Initiated Misfit	Internally Initiated Misfit
Inability to respond to major environmental changes (e.g., to envision an alternative strategy or an alternative structure)	Extending the organization beyond its operating limits (e.g., diversifying beyond the limits of managerial know-how)
Unwillingness to respond to major environmental changes (e.g., to give up enough operating control to diversify)	Modifying strategy and/or structure far enough to violate the organization's operating logic (e.g., centralizing key resources in a divisionalized firm)

hasten their own demise through decisions and actions so at odds with the demands of their environments that it almost appears they "just don't get it."

Why are firms slow to respond, or why are they unwilling or unable to make all the adjustments necessary to respond? Why are other companies seemingly so perverse that their responses run directly counter to those required? Some firms are slow to move—even resistant to the idea that they need to move—because they are captives of their own past success. Market leaders may hesitate to make changes simply because they have the most to lose. Other firms either vacillate in their responses or make incomplete adaptations (e.g., they make a strategic change without the modifications in structure and process necessary to carry it out). We call these latter firms "Reactors," and organizations in this category are found in most industry studies. In Chapter 5, we will explore examples of company failure to respond to major external changes.

The second main type of organizational failure is caused not from without but from within. One of the characteristics of fit is that it is always fragile. The fragility of fit stems from the fact that its ingredients are important not only in their own right, but also because of their interaction with the other ingredients. The strategy a successful firm follows is "built into" its structure and process. Its operating logic is supported by its well-incorporated managerial ideology. Thus, managerial moves that affect one aspect of the organization affect them all, whether or not such effects were intended or understood.

We cannot emphasize enough that strategy, structure, process, operating logic, and managerial ideology are closely interconnected. Managerial decisions may have unintended consequences that may even be virtually undetectable in the short run. Other pieces of the organization may accommodate themselves to a decision that causes strain merely by working harder to overcome the minor problems it causes. Without questioning, groups or units adjust in an effort to be good citizens. However, changes that may be only minor irritants can either accumulate into major dysfunctions or produce them through their own interactive effects. Again, to use a sports analogy, the minor adjustment a professional golfer makes in his or her stance to achieve a few more yards of length may not in itself cause problems. However, it may induce a change in the swing plane that in turn leads to a grip change, and before long the early gains may turn into losses in both distance and accuracy.

Surprisingly, it is sometimes the most successful firms, the Hall of Fame companies, that become the most vulnerable to the process of inadvertent unraveling caused by managers' internal changes as they search for even greater success. In fact, numerous examples of such failure can be cited. Several of the more prominent cases will be examined in Chapter 6.

THE DYNAMICS OF MISFIT AND FAILURE

One of the most troublesome aspects of misfit and failure is that the process by which they occur is incremental, interactive, and cumulative. If harmful changes occur over a long enough period, both the changes and the adaptations made to them may well become so deeply ingrained in the organization that the next generation of managers takes them as givens.

In a firm where prior tight fit has come largely undone, the stated operating logic may bear little relation to the way things actually work. In such circumstances, managers may lose the ability to differentiate between current reality and the historical reputation of their company. For example, managers may refer to their company's structure as "decentralized" long after enough changes have occurred to remove all autonomy from division managers. Or managers may state that their firm values and rewards innovation, despite the fact that research and development funds have been so curtailed that innovation rates and rewards are minimal. Thus, just as success is supported by myths that reinforce its virtues, failure is often accompanied by myths that disguise its vices.

Even more troubling is the growing loss of operating logic in firms that have begun the long slide into misfit. As we have said, managers may come to accept poorly integrated changes as normal, but they may also begin to "learn" from the new system adaptation lessons that generate even more convoluted operating processes over time. Without a clear blueprint designed to achieve tight fit, repairs and tinkering have little chance of leading the company back to a prior level of performance or forward to a new model of success.

In the present transitional period, as in those that occurred before, many firms are spending their time and effort treating the symptoms of underlying ailments. They are caught in the dynamics of misfit and are unaware that their actions may well be driving them deeper into trouble. Worse still, they may have become so entangled in their own mistakes that they can find no starting point for redesign. We will explore these dynamics in depth in the next two chapters and will offer some preventive actions in Part 4.

CHAPTER 5

FAILURE TO
RESPOND TO
EXTERNAL CHANGE

In 1987, IBM's stock price peaked at $176. By 1993, IBM shares were trading regularly in the $40s and $50s. Sales growth at IBM continued through 1989, and operating and net profits were only slightly below record levels as late as 1990. By 1992, however, net losses virtually equalled in absolute size the top earnings figures of earlier years. Total employment at IBM went from a peak in the 400,000 range to less than 300,000 by 1992, with further cuts made in 1993.

How does a Hall of Fame company such as IBM fall so far from grace? In much the same way, though not as far, as those now defunct airline pioneers Eastern and Pan American fell. And in much the same way that tobacco industry stalwarts American Brands and Liggett & Meyers struggled in the 1960s and early 1970s. And, before that, Ford Motor Company in the 1920s and 1930s, and so on.

Like the fallen giants that came before it, IBM has experienced temporary failure because it could not or did not run far enough, fast enough, or in the right direction to keep up with changes in its environment. IBM will likely survive, but whether it will regain the preeminent position it once held depends on how quickly it can stop its current downward spiral and create a new organization that fits its new and continually changing environment.

STRUGGLING TO RESPOND: A RECURRING PROBLEM

To understand the complexity of external trends and events in major transitional periods as well as the difficulties that firms have in responding to them, a brief look at the experiences of several firms in different transitional periods is helpful. Are there patterns in their adaptive behavior that today's firms should either emulate or avoid?

FORD MOTOR COMPANY IN THE 1920s AND 1930s

The experience of few firms so painfully demonstrates the problems of adjusting to external change as does that of the Ford Motor Company in the late 1920s and 1930s. Having demonstrated the benefits of vertical integration in the efficient production of a very limited product line, Ford was understandably reluctant to experiment with technological improvements or the styling changes emerging among its rivals. The long and successful run of the Model T, the driving force in bringing the automobile to a mass market, was followed by the almost equally long and successful run of the Model A, which virtually made an automobile a household necessity.

However, as engineers at General Motors and at the even more adventurous Chrysler Corporation began the process of elevating consumer expectations of variety and new levels of performance, safety, and esthetic design, Ford was reluctant to change its trademark shapes or introduce the product complexity that might threaten its efficient production processes. The single-minded determination of Henry Ford to continue along the path that had brought the company so far gradually turned into a liability. Indeed, it took Henry Ford's removal to change the firm's course.

AMERICAN BRANDS IN THE 1950s THROUGH THE 1970s[1]

In 1950, American Brands produced two of the nation's leading brands of cigarettes, Lucky Strike and Pall Mall, and had captured over 30 percent of the cigarette market. In 1957, four years after the Sloan-Kettering report linking smoking to cancer, American Brands still boasted that its leading brands were among the top three nonfiltered brands, and it developed no significant new brands until the 1960s. As late as 1966, non-filtered cigarettes still accounted for 70 percent of American Brands' sales, while at the same time the industrywide pattern was reversed, with filtered cigarettes accounting for 70 percent of the market, including 91 percent of sales at fast-growing rival Philip Morris.

Two main factors contributed to American Brands' slow response to environmental change. First, the company was naturally hesitant to do anything that might damage the leadership position of its two key brands. Obviously, American Brands had much to lose if its actions and those of its competitors pushed consumers away from these industry icons. Second, the company's Defender strategy had focused for decades on market penetration through heavy advertising expenditures on its two main brands. Compared to most of its smaller rivals, American Brands had little experience with developing and marketing new brands. Thus, not only was the company constrained by its own success, it was also constrained by its lack of expertise in the areas of product design and marketing, skills favored by the new competitive environment.

By 1974, following the U.S. Surgeon General's report of 1964 and the broadcast advertising ban of 1970, American Brands had slipped to fourth place in industry sales and continued to have one of the industry's highest failure rates in new brand introductions (particularly of filter brands). In contrast, the industry's Prospector, Philip Morris, had the highest number of new brand attempts, coupled with one of the lowest failure rates, while doubling its share of the market. Predictably, the Analyzer, R.J. Reynolds, had even fewer failures. Only after American Brands changed its CEO was it able to achieve a small change in its product mix, but even that response was not able to overcome the company's lack of expertise in the design and introduction of new brands.

AMERICAN TELEPHONE & TELEGRAPH
IN THE 1980s

The fact that American Telephone & Telegraph had difficulty responding to a dramatic shove into the turbulence of a competitive marketplace should in no way be surprising. Despite the company's reputation for technical excellence, and the fact that it and its operating subsidiaries had created the world's best telephone system, AT&T had had little reason to develop expertise in monitoring and responding to market forces. The protection provided by its monopoly position allowed AT&T and its subsidiaries to control the pace of technological change and thus focus a vast integrated organization on operating and cost efficiency. AT&T and its operating subsidiaries were, in fact, a centrally planned economy.

Moreover, in their earliest moves, many of the former Bell System companies behaved as erratically as some recently privatized companies in other countries, racing into investment areas for which they were unprepared, putting existing managers in charge of strategies beyond their experience, and generally succeeding only in those areas that tapped into the company's prior core competence. Now, more than a decade after the deregulation decision, AT&T and its former subsidiaries have managed to combine their various business strategies, structures, and processes into a viable organizational form. AT&T is organized into over twenty major business units, and the Baby Bells have forged organizations suited to the characteristics of their respective environments.

IBM IN THE 1980s AND 1990s

In many ways, the closest corporate analogy to IBM in the early 1980s was AT&T. IBM in the early days of the computer revolution so dominated the market for mainframe systems that its standards were those of the industry. Given its commanding position, IBM, like AT&T, could and did control the pace of technological innovation—not by monopoly fiat but by sheer market power coupled with customer respect and dependence. IBM offered widely varied business firms the computer expertise, service, and assurance that they wanted but could not match internally. IBM's more technically oriented customers were less enamored with the pace of its research advances, but remained dependent on the company for parts, service, and system upgrades.

Thus, while it was a private-sector firm with a well-deserved reputation for customer service, IBM, like AT&T, was not a market-driven company—it drove the market. Moreover, its control of technology allowed IBM to integrate the flow of resources across its vast organization and to do so with management systems that maintained the loyalty and enthusiasm of its army of managers and technicians. Although the company was huge and complex, it was stable enough to be understood and to allow the complex coordination mechanisms required by its global matrix to operate effectively.

IBM's problems, like those of AT&T, began in the 1980s as technological advances and global competition began to erode its near monopoly of expertise and service. From a technical perspective, the 1980s were a period of discovery for business, one in which the growing computational and processing power of smaller computers began to interact with increasing ease of use and greater familiarity among users. Thus, external change began to drive parts of the market. IBM was faced increasingly not only with a diminished need for mainframe computers by business but also with a diminished need for its consulting services. Businesses were developing a combination of simpler, user-friendly computer systems and simultaneously reducing their dependence on some types of vendor services.

Throughout the 1970s, IBM could suggest that a customer considering a rival's product wait until the new IBM model came out a year or so later, but by the mid-1980s the market was essentially unwilling to wait. IBM's price structure was now being severely tested and its pace of technological innovation questioned. As IBM sought to speed up its own internal processes, it discovered that what had seemed in a controlled world to be a highly effective structure was now, in an externally dictated world, cumbersome and expensive. As the company headed into the 1990s, it stumbled more and more, and the volume of criticism was turned up as never before.

WHY DON'T FIRMS RESPOND?

Why is it that companies as well managed as IBM was do not spot and react to changes early enough to avoid heavy costs to customers, employees, and stockholders? One major problem facing all firms is that failures such as IBM's tend to occur during periods in which external changes are so pervasive, complex, and revolutionary that they demand not just incremental responses but deep, fundamental redesigns. Thus, even when a firm makes some early incremental responses, it may still be pulled under by the full force of the accumulating change. In addition to this general problem, each firm must also overcome its own particular barriers to effective response. Any one (or more) of four such barriers may stand in the way of a firm's refitting itself to a changed environment (see Table 5–1).

BARRIER 1: STRATEGIC PREDISPOSITION

One major barrier to responsiveness is the predisposition to act in a certain manner that is built into the company's current strategy. For Prospector firms following a first-to-market strategy based on product innovation, changes in consumer taste are generally viewed as an opportunity rather than a threat. It is just such changes that a Prospector trains and staffs itself to anticipate, respond to, and even to lead. On the other hand, Prospectors may not be as alert to changes in process technology, because they do not like to invest in special-purpose capital equipment that lessens their flexibility. The Prospector's response to most change—to innovate, to come up with more design advances—generally succeeds, except in those revolutionary periods when dramatic process advances and their cost-reducing impact demand attention. In the present computer industry, Prospectors have to be alert to process technologies that could lead to lower cost levels.

Conversely, the Defender's focus on efficient production of goods or services makes it especially attentive to advances in process technology but often a laggard in terms of product design innovations. This focus may serve the Defender well, except in times of revolutionary product or service break-throughs. In those periods, Defenders may find that even a large cost advantage is not enough to attract customers to suddenly out-of-date designs. Clearly, this was the problem Ford faced in the 1930s and 1940s as the number of competing car models grew. More recently, in the computer printer and copier busi-nesses, design changes in the past five years have been so dra-matic that the 1990 product lines of standard, low-cost, reliable offerings are now out of date. Defenders have been forced to add standard features that were major new design options only a few years before. In most instances, as American Brands' expe-rience shows, Defenders have unfortunately neither developed nor acquired the expertise necessary for major product innova-tion and development.

Analyzers, those companies that follow Prospectors into promising areas with the intent to produce a better product at a lower price, have a distinctive competence in combining prod-uct and process innovations. Analyzers know how to move a few new products or services from the project phase to efficient production through a carefully coordinated sequence. However, Analyzers are especially challenged by unusually fast-paced change at either the product or process level. The need for rapid adaptation strains and may damage the complex, lateral flow of people and other resources across organizational units. This was exactly the organizational problem that IBM faced in the 1980s, both domestically and internationally.

Reactors, firms that lack a stable strategic focus or whose strategies are not supported by structures and processes that fit, are of course unable to cope effectively with external change. In periods of minor change, Reactors may catch up fast enough to avoid complete failure, but in revolutionary periods, the true

Table 5–1
REASONS FIRMS FAIL TO RESPOND TO ENVIRONMENTAL CHANGE

Reason	Typical Rationale
Strategic predisposition	"What we're good at doing is not what the market wants"
Burden of market leadership	"We didn't get to be No. 1 by not knowing what the market wants" or "We have too much to lose by making changes we may not have to make"
Managerial philosophy	"Those kinds of adaptation will cause too many problems in how we manage"
Tightening downward spiral	"I see no alternatives—maybe we must simply try harder"

weaknesses of Reactor firms are exposed. For example, a study of the airline industry prior to deregulation pointed to an unusually high proportion of self-acknowledged Reactors, firms whose managers recognized their lack of strategy, structure, and process fit.[2] Predictably, when deregulation removed the protective umbrella of federal route and price approval, an almost immediate rash of airline failures and ultimate bankruptcies occurred. Similarly, in the tobacco industry, a company widely viewed as having a poor internal and external fit, Liggett & Meyers, suffered heavily in the transitional period.

In sum, inertia caused by a company's current strategic direction makes it difficult for that company to act confidently and aggressively outside its domain of competence.

BARRIER 2: THE BURDEN OF MARKET LEADERSHIP[3]

Being an industry leader is a two-edged sword. Market leaders usually have the resources to smooth out minor transitions and to survive a crisis that might destroy smaller, less endowed competitors. Nevertheless, industry leadership can inflict its own wounds in periods of major transition. In such periods, the industry pacesetter may be slower to respond to change than its currently smaller peers.

One reason is that dominance breeds confidence (and perhaps arrogance, too). Market leaders have demonstrated their know-how and have been rewarded for it. However, if a transition favors a new approach, leaders may be understandably reluctant to acknowledge the need to respond. That is, the leader's current prowess, like a bodybuilder's overdeveloped muscles, may limit its flexibility. Market leaders may be tempted to respond to major transitions by making minor adjustments that do not threaten their basic approach, or by merely trying harder to make their previously successful system work under the new conditions. Such efforts seriously delayed effective responses by Swiss watchmakers to the challenge of electronic watch technology in the 1970s. Similarly, IBM in the 1980s to some extent stayed with organizational structures and management processes more suited to the period of mainframe computing than to the developing world of minicomputers and microcomputers.

Another reason market leaders may be slow to respond to change is that they have the most to lose if a new approach comes into being. The leader's position has been developed in a particular context, one in which competitors are known and understood, customer relationships are strong and stable, supply and distribution channels are set, and so on. A fundamental change in this configuration represents an opportunity for the firms below and a threat to those on top. The smaller rival has less to lose and the most to gain by quickly trying new approaches in major transitional periods, when the total industry is changing. Just such a pattern occurred—the leader falling and the challengers rising toward the top—in the tobacco industry following the U.S. Surgeon General's 1964 report on the dangers of smoking. Philip Morris and R.J. Reynolds took market share from American Brands and have not been threatened by that company since.

Again, dominant industry leaders have cultures and procedures not amenable to revolutionary environmental change. Sometimes they cannot react adeptly or fast enough by doing business as usual with incremental adaptations.

BARRIER 3: MANAGERIAL IDEOLOGY

As we will explore in greater depth in Chapter 9, managers' own ideologies may be the largest barrier their companies face in responding to some forms of external change. For example, recall that Sears, Roebuck President Wood, as he put forth his plan for a nationwide chain of retail stores, had to overcome his own top managers' doubts that local store managers could operate effectively thousands of miles away from corporate control. Similarly, Henry Ford's reluctance to delegate virtually any decision making outside his collection of close friends was a barrier to that firm's responsiveness.

Moreover, it is not always the most archaic management philosophies that stand in the way of new strategy-structure-process approaches. Managers with human relations views popular from the 1930s to the 1960s may have the greatest difficulty with strategies or structures that demand either joint decision making or true delegation. They have learned to use participative techniques without fully tapping into subordinates' abilities, limiting delegation to routine matters. Human relations-oriented managers may not be able to differentiate their paternalistic maneuvers from the real changes in philosophy that are required. In fact, it is common for human relations managers to claim that their subordinates have far more influence and autonomy than their subordinates believe they actually have.

The newer organizational forms are heavily predicated on deep and wide human know-how and competence. Managers who do not believe in employees' abilities and know-how, and who are therefore unwilling to delegate decision making to them, are a major barrier to successful adaptation.

BARRIER 4: THE TIGHTENING DOWNWARD SPIRAL[4]

When a company's responses to external change are so lacking that it heads into a serious decline, several dysfunctional behaviors may occur, some almost uncontrollably. Just as a driver may panic and lock the brakes or jerk the steering wheel in the wrong direction when the car begins to slip on a wet surface, or a pilot may put a stalling airplane into an even worse aerodynamic position, managers can make damaging changes by not fully understanding their consequences. For example, several U.S. textile firms cut back dramatically on capital investments and research and development expenditures in cost-savings efforts to meet the prices of foreign competitors. These actions in fact reduced their long-term competitive capabilities.

Deepening declines may also result in vacillation among alternatives, so swiftly begun and shifted that no clear course is charted. Alternatively, managers may be driven into near paralysis by their inability to choose among overanalyzed but undertested alternatives. These sorts of behaviors were demonstrated by Pan American and other failing airlines as their slide toward failure steepened.

Finally, as the downward spiral tightens, even large firms lose the resources they need to adapt. In fact, the indiscriminant across-the-board cuts in management and technical personnel common in recent years have subsequently restricted the strategic options open to many firms. And, of course, large losses make it difficult for firms to generate the energy and courage needed to launch major new investment-based strategies. Further pressure is put on companies by large stockholders and stock analysts when predictions about the companies' declining profitability or losses cause further erosion of stock prices.

CAN RESPONSE BARRIERS BE LOWERED?

Given the problems even successful firms face in transition periods, the key question must be, "Can these barriers be lowered?" The answer is yes—but not easily.

Firms can take out "insurance" against the natural risks of their current strategies. Defenders, for example, can acquire a subsidiary whose core competence is product design, which can then license to the parent firm the production of new products as they become viable. The danger, of course, is that the Defender parent will intrude on the operations of the subsidiary and constrain its responsiveness. Similarly, Prospectors can acquire and learn from a manufacturing or parts-producing subsidiary, allowing it to produce for both the parent and outside clients and to compete on the basis of cost efficiency. Again, parent-firm policies will not likely fit those needed in the subsidiary, and true autonomy must be maintained. Analyzers can experiment with lateral resource-allocation mechanisms that speed up decision making to meet changing market conditions as, for example, some firms use internal markets to guide resource flows among units.

We suggested just such "insurance policies" in the late 1970s,[5] but, for most firms, either the benefits did not appear to outweigh the costs or managers were unable to implement the concept. Today, however, such insurance policies may be taken out as a natural component of effectively designed network structures (which we will discuss in Chapters 7 and 8).

No obvious mechanism is available to ease the burden of market leadership, the barrier industry leaders face by having the most to lose if revolutionary change occurs. On the other hand, one benefit of market leadership is the generation of large and continuing resources, a portion of which can be invested in scanning and experimenting. Today, some successful firms are experimenting with programs of intrapreneurship to spur the evaluation and implementation of new ideas. Market leaders must continually remind themselves that it is easier to change when it isn't necessary. Thus, devil's advocacy, counter-intuitive ideas, disagreement, and perhaps even heresy are encouraged in healthy organizations.[6]

Managerial ideologies create some of the largest barriers many firms face, barriers that are difficult to lower or remove because they are not easily recognized for what they are. Indeed, few managers think through their own managerial philosophies or the manner in which these may inhibit or enhance strategy, structure, or process options. The relationship between organizational form and managerial ideology is discussed in Chapter 9, including the philosophical barriers to the adoption of the network form. Network structures highlight the relationship between form and philosophy—in fact, they specifically test managers' willingness to substitute investments in the development of trust for investments in the mechanisms of control.

In sum, unlike many writers and consultants today, we are not convinced that the only way for firms to respond to major environmental change is by changing leaders—tossing out members of the top management team as was done at General Motors and IBM.[7] In fact, while major transitions demand major responses, there is no guarantee that new management teams will bring with them knowledge and understanding of the new recipe needed to be successful. Indeed, it is our view that neither insider teams nor outside replacements are likely to succeed without explicitly exploring the internal and external fits of a new organizational form, as well as the managerial philosophy required to energize and maintain it. We will return to this point, and offer a number of recommendations, in Part 4.

CHAPTER 6

UNRAVELING
FROM WITHIN

We have described how firms may fail to keep pace with changes in their environment and thereby lose the external fit necessary to be successful. There is another class of actions, however, that may result in misfit or failure, but these arise from within the organization. Managerial decisions and behaviors of this sort are particularly insidious because they usually occur incrementally and their consequences are unintended. In fact, managers take these actions in the belief that they are helping their organizations.

One main class of managerial "mistake" can be called the "extension failure." It occurs when managers make a series of decisions that separately are logical but in the aggregate push an organizational form beyond the limits of its capability. The other type of mistake is the "modification failure." Here managers make changes to the organization that appear to be reasonable on the surface but in actuality violate the form's operating logic. Neither of these mistakes can be completely avoided, since both result from rational actions taken by managers in pursuit of increased organizational effectiveness. The only means of minimizing the negative impact of such actions is a deep understanding of how the various organizational forms work, so that as extensions and modifications are made, their full implications for organizational effectiveness are examined in advance.

In this chapter, we will first discuss extension and modification failures in each of the three main organizational forms (functional, divisional, and matrix). We will show, through a series of well-known company examples, how each of the forms can be unraveled from within by well-intentioned managers who make decisions that are individually supportable but collectively damaging. Then, using the concept of internal unraveling, we will return to currently successful companies such as Wal-Mart, Rubbermaid, and General Electric to illustrate future failure scenarios—which, of course, we hope will not occur.[1]

UNRAVELING FIT IN THE FUNCTIONAL FORM

As described earlier, the functional organization can be thought of as a special-purpose machine designed to produce a limited line of goods or services in large volume and at low cost. To be successful, the functional organization's specialized skills and equipment must be optimally utilized. Firms in the late nineteenth and early twentieth century frequently integrated forward, creating new wholesaling and retailing channels to ensure that their output was efficiently distributed and sold. Similarly, these firms often integrated backward to ensure the steady flow of materials and components essential to efficient operation.

Although vertical integration assures functionally structured firms of input and output predictability, it does not come without costs. The further backward and forward a firm integrates, the greater the costs of coordination and the larger the number of specialized assets demanding full utilization. Ultimately, it becomes difficult to determine whether any particular asset along the value chain is making a positive contribution to overall profitability. In fact, the recent trend toward disaggregation (e.g., buying rather than making components and outsourcing sales or distribution) reflects the recognition by many functionally organized firms that coordination costs and asset underutilization seriously offset the benefits of predictability and hierarchical control (see Table 6–1).

An early, dramatic example that illustrates these tradeoffs is Ford Motor Company. For a lengthy period beginning in the

Table 6–1
CAUSES OF FAILURE IN TRADITIONAL ORGANIZATIONAL FORMS

	Organizational Form		
	Functional	**Divisional**	**Matrix**
Primary Application	Efficient production of standardized goods and services	Related diversification by product or region	Assets shared between standardized products and prototype contracts (e.g., many aerospace firms) Assets shared between worldwide product divisions and country-based marketing divisions (e.g., some global firms)
Extension Failure	Vertical integration beyond capacity to keep specialized assets fully loaded and/or to evaluate contributions	Diversification (or acquisitions) outside area of technical and evaluative expertise	Expanding number of temporary contracts beyond ability of allocation mechanisms Search for global synergy limits local adaptability
Modification Failure	Product or service diversification that overloads central planning mechanisms	Corporate interventions to force coordination or obtain efficiencies across divisions	Modifications that distort the dual focus (i.e., favor one type of market or product over another)

Reproduced from Raymond E. Miles and Charles C. Snow, "Causes of Failure in Network Organizations." Copyright © 1992 by The Regents of the University of California. Reprinted from the *California Management Review*, Vol. 34, No. 4. By permission of The Regents.

1920s and extending into the 1950s, Ford was one of the most vertically integrated companies in America. Its holdings included iron-ore mines, steel companies, automobile design and manufacturing units, and retail car dealerships. Such integration was a great advantage in producing Ford's narrow product line during its early years, but this organizational approach became increasingly unwieldy and ultimately had to be largely undone when the company sought to diversify its automobile line. Similarly, in the early 1980s, Harley-Davidson discovered that its production inflexibility and excessive costs were a result of attempting to produce virtually all of its own parts and components. Its move to a just-in-time inventory system allowed the company to outsource many parts and supplies, thereby reducing its total cycle time—bringing new products to the market more quickly while lowering overall costs.

What is interesting about managerial mistakes such as those at Ford and Harley-Davidson is that managers are not doing anything wrong—extending a functional structure through forward and backward integration makes perfectly good sense. Rather, such systems frequently fail later on because managers have done too many step-at-a-time things right!

Alternatively, a functional organization will also fail if it is modified inappropriately. The functional organization's logic of centrally controlled, specialized assets does not easily adapt to product or service diversity. A functionally structured manufacturing firm can efficiently produce a limited array of products if demand for the various products can be forecast and production runs strictly scheduled. However, if the number of different products offered becomes too large, or if outside uncertainties interfere with efficient scheduling, the functional form begins to prove inflexible and costly to operate.

For example, Canadian-Pacific, one of the largest companies in Canada today, began as a railroad. Its functional organization was well suited to the running of a railroad, but its centralized structure and management systems became overloaded as the company grew through an ambitious acquisition program. By the 1980s, Canadian-Pacific had over eighty subsidiary companies in its corporate portfolio. However, it tried to use in each of these companies a human resource management system (training, pay, benefits, etc.) that was a modification of the original approach used on the railroad. Eventually, the company realized that its organizational form could not be modified any further and that it had to adopt a new (more divisionalized) form.

CAUSING INTERNAL DAMAGE IN THE DIVISIONAL FORM

The divisional organization is a collection of similar special-purpose machines, each independently operated to serve a particular market. On the basis of economic performance, each is evaluated centrally for possible expansion, contraction, or redirection. As described earlier, the divisional organization at General Motors offered for distinct markets different automobile models, differentiated primarily by price. Similarly, DuPont identified different types of markets in which its several divisions could use technical and managerial know-how in applied chemistry without corporate interference. Sears, Roebuck challenged managers across the country to operate "hometown stores with nationwide buying power."

Although divisionalized firms are adept at moving incrementally into related areas, they are also vulnerable to overextension. Most divisionalized firms have had the experience of moving into markets that initially appeared to be appropriate but ultimately turned out to fall beyond their area of expertise. Entry into unrelated markets weakens the divisionalized firm's ability at corporate headquarters to appraise performance and make investment decisions. As the firm moves further away from its unique informational base, its decisions become no more efficient, and perhaps even less so, than those the market might make. For example, General Mills, a successful divisionalized firm, at least twice extended itself into areas that proved to be beyond its zone of technical and investment expertise, first into electrical appliances and later into toys and fashion goods. In both cases, the firm recognized its own shortcomings and either divested the divisions or moved back from direct operation.

Divisionalized firms are vulnerable to modifications that begin with good reason but subsequently undermine the form's operating logic. For example, the creation of cross-divisional committees to share technology, or of a corporate staff group to help coordinate process improvements, may genuinely prove valuable. However, excessive coordination requirements across divisions eventually constrain the divisions' flexibility in meeting the demands of their respective markets. Similarly, corporate staff enforcement of interdivisional planning gradually undermines corporate management's ability to assess the individual effectiveness of each division. Both types of modifications, though effective when carefully applied, may expand until they violate the logic of divisional independence and corporate appraisal. Just such extensive coordination requirements constrained, in fact destroyed, the operating autonomy of the separate automobile divisions of General Motors. Initially, during a period of mild competition from the early 1950s through the late 1960s, the firm enjoyed cross-divisional scale economies without major losses from decreased flexibility and responsiveness. However, under growing competition in the 1970s, GM's complex interdivisional planning process delayed new product development. Its intrusive coordination mechanisms contributed to unit costs above those of its competitors. Later, in order to produce a "truly new" car (Saturn), GM had to circumvent its own convoluted structure by creating an entirely new division.

Clearly, in a divisionalized firm, broad operating freedom creates the opportunity for divisions to suboptimize—to take actions that improve their own profitability at the expense of possible overall corporate gains. However, such a possibility is merely one of the normal costs of using the divisional form, and it is offset in the longer run by the benefits gained from well-made local decisions. Unfortunately, fewer and fewer firms today appear to be willing to leave the logic of the divisional form intact. Indeed, many firms that refer to themselves as divisionalized in fact have extensive corporate staff coordination and minimal divisional autonomy. Such operations actually produce all the costs and rigidity of the functional form while adding the cost of divisional duplication of resources. Again, individually sound decisions may add up over time, resulting in operating inefficiencies and ineffectiveness.

OVERLOADING THE MATRIX FORM

As with the functional and divisional forms, the matrix organization can be overloaded by extending a firm's operations beyond the capability of its structure. For example, in an aerospace matrix such as that of TRW, McDonnell-Douglas, or Raytheon, each additional project places new demands on the resource allocation capacity of the firm. Ultimately, resources are held but are not kept fully employed, and the firm may achieve something akin to negative synergy—each new logical addition brings with it coordination costs that exceed its benefits.

Equally troublesome are failures of the matrix organization resulting from modifications that violate its operating logic. Recall that the purpose of the matrix is to let two different types of market forces help shape the operation of the firm. However, many firms are unwilling or unable to maintain a balance between or among their market foci and functional components. For example, if worldwide product divisions have no means of influencing the marketing priorities of national or regional marketing groups, operating efficiency may be totally subordinated to local responsiveness. Throughout its history, Unilever has battled this problem. Its strong local organizations have tended to dominate corporate efforts to achieve regional or global efficiencies. Alternatively, if managers of functional departments have full say over assignments to project teams, the needs of the stable portion of the organization will dominate those of the flexible side, making it difficult for project team managers to meet customer needs for both technical sophistication and timeliness. Battle lines and protective ground stances often put stable and flexible sides of the matrix in conflict. As in a bad marriage, there is no easy final authority in decision making.

FAILURE SCENARIOS FOR HEALTHY FIRMS

It may be difficult to imagine that managers in today's most highly successful firms could make the sort of modification or extension mistakes described above. It may be even more difficult to imagine these kinds of mistakes having been made at General Motors and Sears, Roebuck, companies that Peter Drucker hailed as having found the secret of success not only for the moment but for the future. Those companies, as Drucker portrayed them, had such a clear understanding of what they were doing and why that the possibility of slipping into misfit seemed remote.

Nevertheless, it is likely that some firms enjoying tight fit today—perhaps a Wal-Mart, a Rubbermaid, or a General Electric—will become tomorrow's examples of minimal fit as a result of decisions that appeared both reasonable and valuable, at least on the surface. Indeed, it is possible to write a failure scenario for most successful firms, not simply a list of all the things that might go wrong, but a solid prediction of those specific mistakes that are most likely to occur given the firm's existing organizational form.

For example, as a Defender, Wal-Mart is most vulnerable to modifications that create major strains on the core strengths of its centrally planned functional organization. Thus, one would expect Wal-Mart to be generally leery of diversifying into new market areas. Nevertheless, because it has been so successful, it is likely that Wal-Mart will penetrate most of the available markets that tightly fit its existing competence. One can easily imagine, because it has happened often enough in the past to similarly organized companies, that the search for new investment arenas could carry Wal-Mart into markets that may look highly attractive but fall outside the distinctive competence built into its existing structure and processes. One or two such moves could perhaps be accommodated, but either a major diversification or a series of small ones could place Wal-Mart in the unenviable position of losing the efficiency of its present organization or being forced to adopt a divisional structure suitable to an incrementally adopted diversification strategy.

Conversely, it seems likely that Rubbermaid can continue to innovate across its diverse markets, a strategy harmful to Wal-Mart but one that takes full advantage of Rubbermaid's divisional organization. Is "overdiversification"—an extension error—a possibility for Rubbermaid? It is, for example, in the form of a move into new product areas that are outside the company's current technical competence or that require distribution skills not available in its well-honed management systems. On the other hand, an even more likely failure scenario at Rubbermaid is one in which some subsequent management group unravels the competence of the present organization by searching for cross-divisional efficiencies and/or synergies. Because Rubbermaid's current system works so well, corporate staff groups have the opportunity to focus attention on the system's inherent weakness: the natural redundancy involved in giving each division the resources it needs to respond autonomously to its particular market.

Clearly, it is possible to economize at Rubbermaid—to combine some elements of design and development across divisions or to pull some current divisional activities into a corporate department to standardize procedures and reduce duplication. If nothing else, a coordination committee or two could be formed to share product and process designs across units. No single small move in the interest of economy or synergy is likely to destroy the current organizational fit at Rubbermaid. However, a series of small decisions could certainly do so—removing the possibility of bottom-line measurement of divisional performance and forcing key market decisions upward to corporate management.

Finally, it seems unlikely that General Electric, having just been through the process of redesign, and having fully articulated the logic of its global diversification strategy and its dependence on the decision skills of the managers of its numerous operating units, will now begin to undo what it has so carefully constructed. Surely, GE will not fall victim to modifications that will break down the current strong internal fit across marketing, financial, and other systems. Surely it won't—but clearly it once did. GE has already been through the cycle of redesigning its organization in such a manner that corporate staff micromanaged myriad decisions at the divisional level, creating a top-heavy, poorly responding organization that was gaining the benefits of neither specialized centralization nor market-responsive decentralization. Indeed, the failure scenario for General Electric, in the current global economy at least, is already written in its own corporate history.

Is Unraveling Inevitable?

Why are these extension and modification failures so common? Can they be lessened and/or prevented? There are two main reasons why such internal failures occur. First, managers make these mistakes because they have not fully internalized the logic of their company's current organizational form. Managers, in fact, tend to "learn" how their organization works by observation and imitation. They merely do the things that appear to work. Thus, without a deep understanding of how and why units are structured as they are, why communication flows and controls are laid out in a given way, why decision criteria and authority are what and where they are, and so on, managers easily make decisions that appear fine on the surface but have dysfunctional consequences they did not, and perhaps could not, have considered.

However, simply clarifying for managers the operating logic of the organization is not enough. That knowledge must be put to work. A second cause of internal unraveling is that structure and process decisions have no natural home in most organizations. A variety of departments make pieces of these decisions, which accumulate into structural adaptations or new management processes. Accounting influences controls, human resources influences rewards, and consultants advise on unit size and location. It is not yet common in most organizations to post and heed warning signs that structure and process changes, however small, may have distant and sizable consequences.

Certainly, firms can and must make decisions that change strategies, structures, and processes, but these decisions should be made with a full understanding of their impact on one another and on the logic of the total organizational form. Moreover, managers should have a clear picture of how far a given adaptation will take them along the line from one organizational form to another. Within limits, adjustments can produce gains. Carried too far, however, they push the total organization into a new way of operating that may not be fully understood and which may not fit the company's competitive strategy. Managers who understand the logic of their organization can lessen, and perhaps even prevent, extension and modification failures.

CONCLUSION

Most of today's managers have not been taught the concept of fit or the operating logic of each of the major organizational forms. But they must be, if they wish to understand and operate the newest form of organization, the network. However, as we shall see in Part 3, the extension and modification frailties of the network form are both predictable and avoidable. In fact, the network form forces managers to consider some of the costs and benefits of structure and process decisions that usually remain hidden today. Whether or not their firms move to the network form, today's broad trend toward reorganizing will give managers a chance to rethink their total organizational fit and, hopefully, avoid the sort of unraveling decisions discussed here.

PART THREE

FUTURE FIT:
The Twenty-First Century Challenge

The network organization, briefly introduced in Chapter 3, is today in widespread use. Nevertheless, it is still evolving, and many of its costs, benefits, and operating requirements have only begun to be closely examined. Part 3 is devoted to helping managers add the network form to their repertoire of organizational approaches—a recipe for strategy-structure-process fit that, if applied in appropriate settings, can be highly successful.

The network form challenges many existing attitudes and demands new management roles and leadership approaches. Each of its major variations has its own operating logic and its own barriers to success and adaptation.

Fortunately, the network form, in all its complexity, is built from familiar components: the structure, process, and logic features of each of the earlier forms. Therefore, we can build on the knowledge of earlier forms to describe the features and logic of the network organization. Moreover, the failure scenarios that networks face—the mistakes that managers can make that damage their ability to respond to change—are related to those of earlier forms and are thus predictable. Of particular importance to the success of this new form is an appropriate managerial philosophy.

Chapter 7 takes a close look at early and recent applications of the three current types of network organizations. It clarifies the three main elements of the network form: the network firm, the multiple firms linked to produce a specific good or service, and the collection of firms available to be linked together. Chapter 8 explores the network's requirement for new managerial roles and describes the triple fit required among the internal characteristics of network firms and the nature of their interaction with other network partners. Equally important, the chapter offers a new metaphor for the network firm: the spherical organization. Chapter 9 presents what we now know and can predict about the shape of a new managerial philosophy essential to further development of the network form. This new approach, which we call the human investment philosophy, has important implications for leadership, job design, and other managerial processes.

CHAPTER 7

THE NETWORK
ORGANIZATION

In Chapter 3, we introduced the network organization and its three main variations: the stable, dynamic, and internal network. In this chapter, we will explore in detail the operation of firms that use each of these network forms, focusing on their operating logic and the dynamics of their success and failure.

The network form of organization emerged in response to a complex, fast-paced competitive environment that is making challenging demands on firms across the global economy. Today's environment requires the efficiency provided by the specialized skills and assets usually associated with the functionally structured Defender firm; the flexibility and responsiveness expected of the Prospector's innovation-oriented teams and divisions; and the Analyzer's ability to shift resources laterally across units. Moreover, firms need the competence to act fast in whatever they do.

In most instances, this new business equation can only be pursued by combining the specialized talents of two or more firms. Moreover, as firms attempt to hold assets that are focused only on limited segments of the value chain, they frequently must interact with numerous partners if they are to keep their resources fully occupied, a necessary condition for cost efficiency. In an increasing number of industries, this means that the typical firm is not only hooked up to a set of network partners, it is also a potential partner for other firms in the industry. We will describe such situations and argue that the entire set of existing and potential relationships among firms in the industry can be called a network organization. And, because the network is an organization, it can and should be managed.[1]

ACTING BIG AND SMALL
AT THE SAME TIME

The simultaneous demands to be efficient, responsive, adaptable, and fast have been met differently depending on whether the firms in a particular setting are small or large. For example, some network organizations, such as those found in the Italian textile industry or Silicon Valley's computer business, have been created almost spontaneously from local conditions. The primary motive of these firms in forming networks is to obtain the advantages of bigness while remaining small. Conversely, large firms typically disaggregate to form their networks. Big companies focus only on those competencies in which they can compete on a world-class basis, and they outsource remaining activities to upstream or downstream partners. Some examples illustrating each of these paths to the network organization will help show how networks emerge.

FROM SMALL TO BIG

One of the most frequently cited examples of networking among small firms involves the "industrial districts" in Italy, where thousands of small firms specializing in various trades both compete and collaborate with each other.[2] Called "diffuse industrialization" or "flexible specialization," clusters of small firms have been formed in businesses as diverse as engineering, ceramic tile, and clothing. For example, one network of fifteen small engineering firms in Modena formed partnerships or invested capital in other small firms in order to develop collective clout in the marketplace. However, each firm remained a separate legal entity with its own work force, facilities, accounting systems, and so on. In this way, each firm can be a small leading-edge specialist but still participate in large-scale projects.

In some cases, firms emerge that act only as brokers in a particular district. The broker firm serves as the connection to the marketplace, receiving orders from customers and purchasing raw materials, but production is subcontracted to small manufacturing firms. Using this type of network arrangement, where one company takes the lead in organizing the others, a broker firm such as Bennetton can compete globally in the clothing business.

An American variant of the Italian industrial districts is seen in California's Silicon Valley.[3] The second-generation computer firms that appeared in Silicon Valley in the 1980s eschewed the organizational model of their predecessors in the 1960s and 1970s. That is, instead of seeking scale and vertical integration, these small and medium-sized enterprises operate as highly focused specialists that link up with each other at key stages of the value chain. For example, small firms have achieved manufacturing flexibility by avoiding the dedicated, high-volume production lines of their larger predecessors. Also, they have taken advantage of electronic design automation (combining advances in computer-aided design, engineering, and testing) so that their chip and systems designers can implement their ideas directly onto silicon, thus accelerating the product development process considerably. Finally, these newer firms often have unbundled the production process. Few firms engage in the entire process of designing, manufacturing, and assembling integrated circuits. Instead, each firm operates as a specialist in only one (or a few) of the stages of production.

By remaining small, each network firm in businesses such as textiles, semiconductors, biotechnology, and a host of others can be maximally responsive. It has fewer bureaucratic procedures that must be overcome in order to respond to requests from customers or network partners. Further, each small network firm is a specialist in a particular technology. It is at the leading edge of its area of expertise and is therefore a prime candidate when other firms need a certain type of technological contribution. At the same time, a small network firm cannot fully meet the needs of the marketplace; it does not possess the range of skills necessary to do so. Thus, it is highly motivated to be a strong player in a multifirm network because customer needs are ultimately met by the total network acting in concert. In general, by participating in networks, small firms are able to achieve the advantages of bigness.

FROM BIG TO SMALL

Another path to network formation is quite different from the spontaneous origins of the small-firm networks in Italy or California. Many network organizations also have been formed in mature industries because older, established companies came to realize that they were too large and cumbersome to respond effectively to the competitive demands of today's environment. Some of the biggest names in the American corporate lexicon were, or currently are, embroiled in efforts to "reinvent" themselves so that they can act small: General Electric, IBM, Westinghouse Electric, American Telephone & Telegraph, and so on. And, just as every other aspect of business is globalizing, so too is reinvention. Thus, the same forces and responses at work in American companies can be found in German companies such as Daimler Benz and Volkswagen, and in Japanese companies such as Mitsubishi Electric and Nissan Motor.

Although bigness has its advantages, the price of bigness—complex internal coordination requirements—has become far too high for many large companies to afford. Consequently, over the last dozen years or so, a familiar pattern has emerged in how large companies go about regaining their responsiveness.[4] Invariably, the first step is downsizing. General Electric was among the first American companies to reduce head count in the early 1980s. It was followed by scores of other large companies, most recently IBM and Philip Morris in the 1990s. Downsizing, however, is little more than going on a corporate diet—it reduces the number of unneeded people but does not get a company in shape. The next step to true reinvention usually is delayering, reducing the number of levels of management hierarchy in order to speed the flow of information and decision making.

Companies that engage in even greater restructuring may organize into more and smaller business units, form cross-functional teams that are responsible for key processes, and design compensation schemes that reward entrepreneurial behavior on the part of their managers and employees. The overall objective of all these changes is to reduce the centralized coordination requirements and create the flexibility necessary to get close to customers and the speed required to meet their demands in a timely fashion.

The result of these moves on the part of large companies is an increasing number of industries being organized along network lines. Big companies locate their "center of gravity" on the industry value chain by performing only those functions that they do best and by outsourcing other operations to smaller specialist firms. Eventually, a complete network forms around each large company, and the entire industry evolves into a web of relationships that itself can be called a network organization.

In sum, in an increasing number of industries today, firms are moving toward network structures. Whether such movement is driven by small firms linking up to achieve market clout or big firms disaggregating to gain more responsiveness, three main forms of network are evident. These can be called stable, dynamic, and internal networks.

THE STABLE NETWORK

The stable network is designed to serve a mostly predictable market by linking together independently owned specialized assets along a given product or service value chain. However, instead of a single vertically integrated firm, the stable network substitutes a set of component firms, each tied closely to a "core" or "lead" firm by contractual arrangements, but each maintaining its competitive fitness by serving firms outside the network (see Figure 7–1).

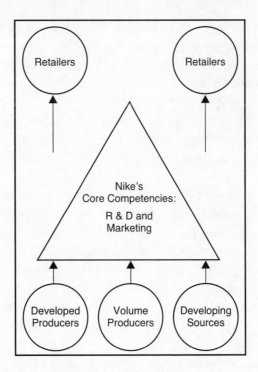

Figure 7–1   Nike: A Stable Network

NIKE INC.[5]

One well-known company that is organized this way is Nike. Nike's core competencies are R&D and marketing. By heavily staffing itself with specialists in biomechanics, exercise physiology, engineering, and industrial design, Nike is able to stay at the forefront in athletic footwear research and development. From its pioneering "waffle" sole introduced in the 1970s to today's exotic shoe colors and designs, Nike has largely dominated product development in this business.

Nike's other main strength is marketing. The company views itself as an "authentic" player in the athletic footwear and apparel industry: former world-class athletes work with current top athletes to design and market the best equipment. This authenticity is surrounded by a vast array of marketing capability. This includes product advertising via contractual arrangements with highly visible athletes such as Michael Jordan, Charles Barkley, and Bo Jackson. It includes a state-of-the-art film production facility at corporate headquarters that makes films and videos for Nike conclaves and marketing events. And it includes a variety of marketing and sports management programs that bring into the Nike stable newer star athletes such as Alonzo Mourning and Rick Mirer as well as entire sports programs at universities such as Miami, North Carolina, and Duke. Nike even markets golf shoes and its own image by operating a professional golf tour.

Nike, however, manufactures only a tiny fraction of its products; this function has never been a significant part of the company's purview—the company began by redesigning and marketing shoes produced by a Japanese firm. Today, manufacturing is done by plants located in Asia, originally in Japan, South Korea, and Taiwan, now increasingly in Indonesia and China. New manufacturing vendors come on line by producing low-end generic footwear like sandals and move to higher-end, more profitable footwear like athletic shoes. Nike works with the best factories in each region, seeking those with the most highly trained work forces, the best development capabilities, and the highest quality production. In addition to upgrading the skills of local employees, Nike works with the footwear industry in each country to develop local material suppliers to service the factories. Here the goal is to have the factories source as many components as possible in each country, enabling Nike to import fewer components and materials from other countries.

Nike's manufacturing operations move periodically. For example, all six Nike-licensed Indonesian plants are managed by South Korean concerns, and none of the machinery used to produce the shoes is made in Indonesia. About 70 percent of the factories' raw materials come from South Korea, where escalating labor costs have made it too expensive to make all but Nike's most technically advanced and expensive shoes. Thus, just as South Korean and Taiwanese plants displaced manufacturing in Japan, a similar transition is occurring from South Korea to Indonesia and on into China.

Nike does not require its manufacturing vendors to produce solely for the company. In fact, Nike allows its factories to produce for competitors such as Reebok and Adidas. Nike believes that the continual upgrading of manufacturing expertise gained by working with multiple partners outweighs disadvantages such as the loss of proprietary knowledge. Moreover, because the factories work with other footwear companies, Nike is not responsible for keeping them fully loaded—which it would have to do if the factories were owned or completely dominated by the company.

Nor does Nike operate the distribution and retailing outlets through which its products are sold. The company sells its products to approximately fifteen thousand retail accounts in the United States and through a mix of independent distributors, licensees, and subsidiaries in approximately eighty countries around the world. As is the case with the manufacturing plants, the distribution and retailing companies also do business with other athletic footwear and apparel firms.

OPERATING LOGIC OF THE STABLE NETWORK

The multifirm network in which Nike is a key element is in many ways an organization. For example, the total network can be thought of as a set of assets dedicated to the athletic footwear and apparel business. Also, Nike and each of its upstream and downstream partners have knowledge of each other's abilities and are, in varying degrees, committed to making the entire value chain operate effectively. Last, there is a willingness among firms throughout the network to interact with each other in a complementary fashion, working cooperatively to improve efficiency and disciplining members whose behavior hurts the network. These network features of purpose, know-how, commitment, and motivation are all necessary ingredients of any successful organization. Similar stable network organizations can be seen at BMW, Motorola, and Corning.

The stable network has its roots in the structure of the functional organization, and therefore its operating logic is *centrally coordinated specialization.* However, instead of employing the vertical integration associated with traditional functional organizations, the network's lead firm outsources its noncore competencies to other specialist firms in order to increase flexibility throughout the network. Thus, Nike specializes in R&D and marketing while the rest of the "organization" performs manufacturing, distribution, and selling.

POTENTIAL CAUSES OF FAILURE IN THE STABLE NETWORK

Given the operating logic of the stable network, the most common threat to its effectiveness is an extension that demands the complete utilization of the supplier's or distributor's assets for the benefit of the lead firm. If the several suppliers and distributors in the stable network focus their assets solely on the needs of a single lead firm, the benefits of broader participation in the marketplace are lost. Unless suppliers sell to other firms, the price and quality of their output is not subject to market test. Similarly, unless multiple outlets are used, the value actually added by distributors must be set by judgment rather than by market-driven margins. The process of asset overspecialization and overdedication by network partners is frequently incremental and can therefore go unnoticed. Continued, step-by-step customization of a supplier's processes, either voluntarily or at the lead firm's insistence, can ultimately result in the inability of the supplier to compete in other markets and an obligation on the part of the lead firm to use all of the supplier's output (see Table 7–1).

Another reason for network members to participate in the market outside their relationship with the lead firm is to force these components to maintain their technological expertise and flexibility. Suppliers come into contact with innovations in product or service design, and develop their adaptive skills, by serving various clients. Overspecialization and limited learning can easily occur if both the lead firm and its components are not alert. In fact, for maximum effectiveness, both the lead firm and its network partners must explicitly consider the limits of allowable dedication—forcing themselves to set restrictions on the proportion of a partner's assets that can be utilized.

The stable network can also be damaged by unthoughtful or even inadvertent modifications. In the search for assurance that suppliers will meet quality standards and delivery dates, some lead firms attempt to specify the processes that the network partner must use. Deep involvement in a supplier's or distributor's processes can occur through innocent zeal on the part of the lead firm's staff and may even be endorsed by the staff of the network partner. Within limits, close cooperation to ensure effective linkage is valuable. However, the lead firm can ultimately find itself "managing" the assets of its partners and accepting responsibility for their output. Moreover, when the operating independence of the network member is severely constrained, any creativity that might flow from its managers or staff is curtailed and the lead firm does not get the full benefit of the partner's assets. In effect, in its zeal to insure compliance with its needs, the lead firm is reconverting the network into a vertically integrated functional organization, with all of its attendant rigidities.

THE DYNAMIC NETWORK

In faster-paced competitive environments, firms form networks that are very dynamic. For the dynamic network to achieve its full potential, there must be numerous firms (or units of firms) operating at each point along the value chain, ready to be pulled together for a given product or venture and then disassembled to become part of another strategic alliance. Businesses such as apparel, toys, and biotechnology may require or allow firms to outsource extensively. In such circumstances, the lead firm identifies and assembles assets owned largely (or entirely) by other companies. Lead firms themselves typically rely on only a limited set of core competencies such as manufacturing, design, or marketing and service.

Table 7–1
CAUSES OF FAILURE IN NETWORK ORGANIZATIONS

	Type of Network		
	Stable	**Internal**	**Dynamic**
Operating Logic	A large core firm creates market-based linkages to a limited set of upstream and/or downstream partners	Commonly owned business elements allocate resources along the value chain using market mechanisms	Independent business elements along the value chain form temporary alliances from among a large pool of potential partners
Primary Application	Mature industries requiring large capital investments; varied ownership limits risk and encourages full loading of all assets	Mature industries requiring large capital investments; market-priced exchanges allow performance appraisal of internal units	Low-tech industries with short product design cycles and evolving high-tech industries (e.g., electronics, biotechnology)
Extension Failure	Overutilization of a given supplier or distributor leading to unhealthy dependence on core firm	Extending asset ownership beyond the capacity of the internal market and performance appraisal mechanisms	Expertise may become too narrow and role in value chain is assumed by another firm
Modification Failure	High expectations for cooperation can limit the creativity of partners	Corporate executives use "commands" instead of influence or incentives to intervene in local operations	Excessive mechanisms to prevent partners' opportunism or exclusive relationships with a limited number of upstream or downstream partners

Reproduced from Raymond E. Miles and Charles C. Snow, "Causes of Failure in Network Organizations." Copyright © 1992 by The Regents of the University of California. Reprinted from the *California Management Review*, Vol. 34, No. 4. By permission of The Regents.

THE COMPUTER INDUSTRY:
HOME OF THE MODULAR CORPORATION[6]

The computer industry offers a hospitable environment for the operation of numerous dynamic networks. One such successful network is led by Dell Computer Corporation, a downstream player in the personal computer business.[7] Dell's strengths are in customer-driven technology, marketing, and service. In less than a decade, Dell has made huge inroads into the PC market against larger and better known competitors such as IBM, Apple, Compaq, and Digital Equipment Corporation. It has done so through an organizational arrangement that relies heavily on the rapid formation and utilization of key strategic alliances.

Dell sells an ever-expanding array of customized personal computers directly to customers who read about the products in newspaper ads or catalogs. Customers can specify their desired monitor, microprocessor, and a variety of other options. This is the essence of Dell's customer-driven technology, a successful direct-marketing model that Dell pioneered in the PC business. Dell owns no manufacturing plants; it leases two small factories (in Texas and Ireland) to assemble computers from outsourced parts. Instead of doing its own manufacturing, Dell invests heavily in training its salespeople and service technicians. The productivity of these employees is among the highest of any personal computer company and compares favorably to that of the best discount retail stores.

The remainder of Dell's "modular" organization is a set of other firms with which Dell has formed more or less temporary alliances. For example, several microprocessors used in the company's products are currently available only from Intel Corporation, and Dell has other ongoing single-supplier relationships that are considered advantageous for price and quality reasons. On the other hand, the company employs numerous contract sources for components and assembly when and where they are needed. In the past few years, Dell has accelerated its program of international expansion with the goal of creating a global network organization. For example, it signed a sales agreement

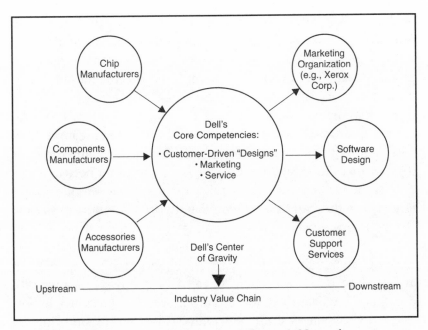

Figure 7–2   Dell Computer: A Dynamic Network

with one of India's largest PC manufacturers to market Dell products in that country, and it continues to build sales in South and Central America and the Caribbean through an ongoing distribution agreement with Xerox Corporation.

Most recently, Dell has decided to branch out from the DOS-based PC market to sell bigger and more powerful computers that run Unix operating systems. Here again, Dell's organizational approach is that of a network. It teamed up with UniDirect Corporation, a small new firm that specializes in computer software and customer support services for Unix operating systems. UniDirect uses its contacts in the Unix market, making arrangements with software vendors to provide partially activated programs that Dell preloads at its factory. The result is that Dell can offer a "mass customized" medium-size computer to a new market segment.

In a different part of the computer industry resides Novell Inc., another leader of a dynamic network organization.[8] Novell is the market leader in networking software, programs that link together masses of personal computers into "local-area networks." Many firms, along with Novell, believe that large computer systems will eventually be replaced by cheaper local-area networks and, increasingly, wide-area networks. Novell is trying to remain at the forefront of this transformation. The company's chairman, Raymond Noorda, has initiated a comprehensive strategy of acquisitions, alliances, and new-product development to accelerate the growth of computer networking.

In some ways, Novell's organizational approach looks no different from those of other dynamic network leaders such as Dell. Novell keeps a very clear focus on its core competencies in networking software R&D, and it outsources other activities by forming partnerships with distributors and other companies. In at least two ways, however, Novell is a distinctive leader of a dynamic network. First, Raymond Noorda is a visionary executive who has successfully articulated, both within and outside his company, a view of computing's future that is widely shared. In the high-velocity environment that is the computer industry, vision is an essential ingredient in keeping the various elements of a network organization focused and coordinated. Second, for years Noorda has promulgated a concept that he calls "coopetition." He encourages competing companies to also cooperate, pushing for industry standards and sharing technology. The premise of coopetition is that if the entire industry grows, every competitor will benefit.

OPERATING LOGIC OF
THE DYNAMIC NETWORK

The operating logic of the dynamic network is linked to that of the divisional form of organization. Recall that the divisionalized organization emphasized responsiveness by focusing independently operated divisions on distinct but related markets. The combination of central evaluation (corporate) and local operating autonomy (divisions) is reflected in the dynamic network, in which a lead firm links together independent firms, in alliances of greater or lesser degrees of permanency, to design, manufacture, and sell a particular product or service. Thus, the dynamic network's operating logic is partner-firm independence coupled with the lead firm's overall vision.

POTENTIAL CAUSES OF FAILURE
IN THE DYNAMIC NETWORK

The availability of numerous potential partners eager to apply their skills and assets to the upstream or downstream needs of a given firm is not only the key to success of the dynamic network but also a possible source of trouble. For example, if a particular firm in the value chain overspecializes—refines but over time also restricts its expertise—it runs the risk of becoming a "hollow" corporation, a firm without a clearly defined, essential contribution to make to the network.[9] Firms need to occupy a wide enough segment of the value chain to be able to test and protect the value of their contribution. A design firm needs to retain its ability to build prototypes, a manufacturer may need to experiment with new process technologies, and so on. Firms with a contribution base that is either too narrow or too weakly defined are easily overrun by their upstream and/or downstream neighbors. Indeed, examples abound of firms (and industries) pushed into decline and ultimate failure by excessive outsourcing. From radios to television sets to video recorders, outsourcing decisions by U.S. corporations allowed foreign suppliers to acquire the technical competence to design and sell their own products, eventually capturing the bulk of U.S. domestic markets.

Conversely, firms with a clear competence-based position on the value chain, a base maintained by continuing investment in technology and skill development, can afford to interact confidently with upstream and downstream partners. Nevertheless, there is a constant temptation for firms to go beyond the development of their own competence as a means of ensuring their viability. For example, they may seek to add protection through an excessive concern for secrecy, a legalistic approach to contractual relations, or preferential treatment of particular partners.

Engaging in true coopetition, as preached by Novell, sometimes involves walking a very fine line.

In sum, the dynamic network places demands on its member firms to reappraise continually their technical competence and the scope of their activities, to maintain not only their own well-being but that of the broader network as well. No one firm can know everything that is happening or everything that is needed in the total network. However, each member can preserve its own competence and refrain from behaviors that threaten over-all network performance.

THE INTERNAL NETWORK

The logic of the internal network requires the creation of a market inside a firm. Here a company's various units buy and sell goods and services among themselves at prices established in the open market. Obviously, if internal transactions are to reflect market prices, every unit must have regular opportunities to verify the price and quality of its wares, either by buying and selling outside the firm or by having access to current comparative data on market conditions. The purpose of the internal network, like its organizational predecessor the matrix, is to gain competitive advantage through shared utilization of assets as well as continuing development and exchange of managerial and technical know-how.

For example, the giant multinational firm ABB Asea Brown Boveri[10] has grown rapidly to over $25 billion in revenues and a quarter of a million employees through a concerted program of mergers, acquisitions, and restructurings that has given it unmatched local-global synergy in the electrical systems and equipment market. To this point, ABB has increased shareholder value by thoughtfully specifying the market domain of each of its key organizational units and designing the internal mechanisms by which they can exchange goods and services in mutually beneficial ways under overall market discipline.

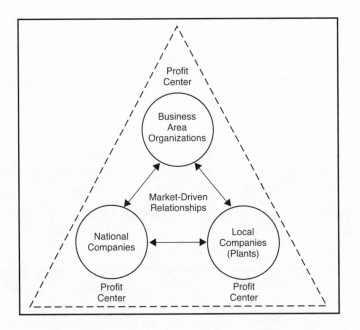

Figure 7–3 ABB: An Internal Network

Headquartered in Zurich, ABB is a young company that resulted from the merger in 1987 of two well-known European firms, Sweden's ASEA and Switzerland's Brown Boveri. Today, ABB is a global federation of approximately thirteen hundred local companies organized so that they can act big and small simultaneously. As a member of the global federation, each company enjoys the advantages and resources of participating in a global business such as power transformers or marine equipment. At the same time, these thirteen hundred companies have on average less than two hundred employees each, and are further organized into five thousand profit centers with an average of fifty employees each. Therefore, each local company is largely a stand-alone operation, with clearly defined responsibilities and considerable freedom to act entrepreneurially in its local marketplace.

The key building blocks of ABB's internal network, which the company refers to as a global matrix, are its sixty-five business areas, its national companies, and its thirteen hundred local companies. One of ABB's businesses, in which it is the world's leader, is power transformers—products used to transmit electricity over long distances. The head of this business area is based in Mannheim, Germany. The production of power transformers takes place in twenty-five factories in sixteen countries. Each of these operations is organized as an independent company with its own president, budget, and balance sheet. Every month, the Mannheim headquarters provides detailed information on how each of the twenty-five plants is performing (throughput times, inventories as a percentage of revenues, etc.). These reports stimulate competition for outstanding performance within the ABB network—adding incentives to those already present in the marketplace. Further, highly efficient plants are expected to serve as challenges and models for less efficient operations. ABB's practice is to show local managers what's been achieved elsewhere in the company, make that expertise available, and expect the local operation to make the necessary changes and get up to speed quickly.

Each business area leader is responsible for optimizing the business on a global basis. This means developing a global business strategy, allocating export markets to each factory, and sharing expertise by rotating people among countries, creating multinational teams to solve problems and building an organizational climate of high trust and open communication. Business area leaders must have the vision, cultural sensitivity, and leadership abilities to operate a worldwide business without directly controlling any of ABB's people or other assets. In effect, they are charged with creating an internal market in which the local companies are motivated to participate actively.

Finally, alongside the business area dimension of the global matrix is the country dimension. ABB's operations in the developed world are organized as national enterprises with presidents, balance sheets, income statements, and career ladders. The local companies in a particular country are subsidiaries of the national company. Thus, an ABB country manager can be thought of as the CEO of a multibusiness company. It is the country manager's job to link the operating abilities of that country's local companies to the business strategies led by various business area managers. Of course, such a complicated task cannot be accomplished successfully unless there is a great deal of decision-making discretion embedded in the organization. This is where ABB's internal market is so powerful. Both the national and local companies make decisions that are in their self-interest, rather than following by rote directives and guidelines from a centrally controlled management hierarchy.

OPERATING LOGIC OF THE INTERNAL NETWORK

The operating logic of the internal network flows from that of the matrix form of organization, namely, a dual focus on products and functions. When a company wishes to operate globally, a third dimension is added to the matrix: markets or regions. As these organizing dimensions accumulate, complexity increases dramatically. Today it is generally acknowledged that a global matrix organization cannot operate effectively if it employs the administrative processes associated with the traditional matrix structure. Therefore, instead of attempting to achieve a balance across the three matrix dimensions of products, functions, and markets through plans and hierarchies, some global companies such as ABB form internal networks in which decisions and resource allocations are guided by market forces.[11]

POTENTIAL CAUSES OF FAILURE
IN THE INTERNAL NETWORK

The most common managerial misstep in internal networks is corporate intervention in resource flows or in the determination of transaction prices. Not every interaction in the internal network can and should flow from locally determined supply and demand decisions. Corporate managers may well see a benefit in having internal units buy from another newly built or acquired unit, even though its actual prices are above those of competitors in the marketplace. Such prices may be needed to sort out the operation and develop full efficiency. However, the manner in which corporate management handles such "forced" transactions is a crucial factor in the continuing health of the network. Ideally, corporate executives will manage the internal economy rather than simply dictate the transfer price and process. This can be accomplished by providing a "subsidy" to the start-up unit to allow it to sell at market prices while still showing a profit, or by providing buyers with incentives that keep their profits at the same rates they would enjoy if they were free to buy from lower-priced competitors. Obviously, such subsidies or incentives should be time-bound and carefully monitored to prevent abuse. Although this process is demanding, it serves to protect the logic of market-based internal transactions. Unfortunately, instead of influencing the internal market and preserving the ability to evaluate organizational units on actual performance, many corporate managers "command" unit behaviors and risk destroying agreement on the criteria for performance evaluation.

Despite potential problems associated with managing the complexity of a large internal network, the shift from complex, centrally planned hierarchies to internal market structures is growing. At a 1991 conference, numerous examples were reported of companies building internal networks in organizations ranging from services (Blue Cross/Blue Shield), to materials (Alcoa), to low-tech (Clark Equipment) and high-tech (Control Data) manufacturers.

THE NETWORK ORGANIZATION: CLARIFYING THE CONCEPT

As firms have experienced the need to be simultaneously efficient, flexible, and adaptive, they have turned increasingly to the network form of organization. Networks composed of multiple specialist companies as their key building blocks have been called "modular corporations." Multifirm networks that change their shape often and quickly have been called "virtual corporations." When networks are used as a substitute for bureaucracy-laden, steep management hierarchies, they are referred to as "horizontal corporations."[12]

MAJOR DIFFERENCES BETWEEN TRADITIONAL AND NETWORK ORGANIZATIONS

Whatever their name, network organizations are indeed different from traditional organizations in several respects. First, instead of holding in-house (or under exclusive contract) all the assets required to produce a given product or service, many of today's networks use the collective assets of several firms located at key points along the value chain. Second, networks rely more on market mechanisms than on administrative processes to manage resource flows. However, these mechanisms are not the simple "arm's length" relationships usually associated with independently owned economic entities. Rather, members of the network recognize their interdependence and are willing to share information, cooperate with each other, and customize their product or service—all to maintain their position within the network. Third, while networks of subcontractors have been common in the construction industry for years, many recently designed networks expect a much more proactive role among their members—voluntary behavior that improves the final product or service rather than simply fulfilling a contractual obligation. Finally, in an increasing number of industries, including venerable vertically integrated manufacturing businesses such as steel, automobiles, and chemicals, networks are evolving that possess characteristics similar to the Japanese *keiretsu*—an organizational collective based on cooperation and mutual shareholding among a group of manufacturers, suppliers, and trading and finance companies.

The rise of the network form has created the need for a new vocabulary to describe organizational behavior in a particular business or industry. In an increasing number of industries—particularly those that are blending together, such as telecommunications, electronics, and broadcasting—the number and complexity of multifirm networks make it difficult to describe and understand the organizational arrangements that are being adopted. If such networks are to be managed effectively, it is imperative to have a clear concept of today's network organization.

Our conception of a network organization is shown in Figure 7–4. In this formulation, a network organization contains three main elements. The first is a "network firm" located at some point along an industry value chain. The network firm is likely to specialize in a few core competencies: Nike in R&D and marketing, Dell in customer-driven technology, and so on. When various network firms team up with each other to operate a business, this set of companies constitutes an "activated network." These companies are partners—members of a variety of strategic alliances of greater or lesser permanence. Last, all the firms, whatever their current linkage, represent a network of "potential partners." This set of firms is constantly being added to as the network reaches out to members of different value chains, seeks out and builds the competencies of members of minor activated networks, and so on. As long as actual and

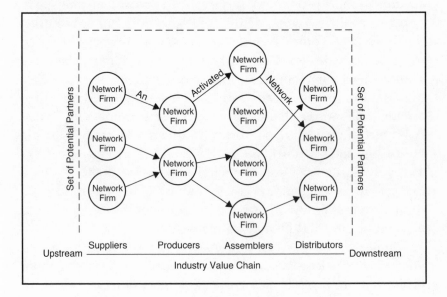

Figure 7–4   A Complete Network Organization

potential network firms have knowledge of each other's abilities, and a willingness and commitment to interact in a complementary fashion, the total collection of activated and potentially activated networks has the properties of an organization.

ORGANIZATIONAL PROPERTIES AND MANAGERIAL REQUIREMENTS

Given that each of the elements described here is an organization, all must simultaneously receive managerial attention. Managers must assist firms, activated networks, and the total network in a manner that enhances their responsiveness to market demands. A brief look at the organizational properties and managerial requirements of each of these elements is useful.

The network firm, as indicated, is likely to be smaller than its non-network counterparts because it focuses its competence on those activities to which it can make the greatest contribution along the value chain. To succeed it must be managed in a manner that keeps its technical competencies current and its management know-how responsive to market changes. In addition, however, the network firm must maintain and enhance its ability to respond flexibly and efficiently to the needs of current and potential network partners. Moreover, as we will explore in more detail in Chapter 8, it must accept the responsibility to help other network firms maintain their technical and adaptive competency.

During the period in which two or more firms are linked to produce a given good or service, the activated network thus created has clear organizational properties. Each of the firms is expected to provide a customized response to the needs of its value-chain partners—a response that reflects its distinctive competence. Moreover, responses to partners must be timely and efficient. Firms cannot attempt to exploit one another or impose costly conditions on their association. It is the task of managers, as we will discuss in Chapter 8, to assist market forces in these exchanges. Managers from all the activated firms add value to their network by sharing information and expertise, demonstrating goodwill and trustworthiness, and making certain their firms meet and exceed all their responsibilities.

The total set of firms arrayed along the value chain from which the partners for activated networks are drawn also has organizational properties. The firms in this broader pool do not view themselves as completely independent—they identify with and feel obligations toward other current and potential network partners. Because they accept their membership in the network, they accept the obligations of that role—the requirements of good citizenship that include not only sharing information but also making referrals to other business firms with more appropriate expertise, locating and recruiting new members for the network, and assisting them in learning network values. The total network adds value beyond pure market exchanges as it learns to operate without exclusionary behaviors and to compete without seeking unfair advantages. This does not occur automatically; it is a managerial responsibility.

CONCLUSION

It is obvious from our descriptions and examples that network organizations demand roles, responsibilities, and competencies that go well beyond those of earlier organizational forms. In Chapter 9, we explore these roles in depth and offer a new way of conceptualizing the structure and management processes within the network firm of the future.

CHAPTER 8

TRIPLE FIT:

Network Roles and the Spherical Form

In the previous chapter, we described the various forces that have pushed mature as well as new industries toward one or the other of the major network forms of organizing. In this chapter, we turn our attention to the mechanisms by which required fit is achieved at all three levels of the network form: across the entire network organization, among network firms in activated organizations, and within each of the specific network firms.

Tight fit at the level of the total network, as well as within the set of firms activated for the delivery of a particular product or service, is achievable only to the extent that managers learn a demanding new set of roles and behaviors. At the level of the individual network firm, the task of achieving fit is even more challenging. The network firm, we contend, can achieve a fit across the network organization no better than its own internal fit. The full potential of network firms, we believe, can only be achieved by adopting a totally new way of conceiving and organizing work—the spherical structure. Finally, if the new network managerial roles are understood and practiced, and if network firms utilize the agility of the spherical structure, the total network will not only enjoy tight fit but become a self-energized and self-renewable enterprise.

NEW MANAGEMENT ROLES

Historically, new organizational forms have required managers to take on different roles and behaviors. For example, in the divisional form, corporate managers had to learn how to perform an investment banking role, fueling divisions with appropriate financial resources to accomplish their goals. In the matrix organization, managers had to learn how to help functional and project units share resources without dictating the outcome. Similarly, today's network organizations have brought to light three managerial role requirements that go beyond those found in earlier forms.[1]

THE DESIGNER ROLE—THE NETWORK ARCHITECT

Networks don't just happen—even those that seem to appear spontaneously in certain settings, such as the Italian textile industry and Silicon Valley's computer business. Someone (or some group) recognizes a need or opportunity and makes the first move to share resources across firms. Someone sees beyond one complementary transaction to the benefits of a continuing interaction along the value chain. Someone envisions and articulates the shape of a broader collective of firms with unique features for the market and mutual benefits for its internal members. And so on. In short, some individuals play an architectural role—they design the network.

At one level, the architect's role is simply that traditionally played by the entrepreneur who sees both a market opportunity and the set of resources needed to respond to it. In some networks, however, the architect may go well beyond the entrepreneur's normal focus and activities. This might include not only envisioning but even creating the resources necessary to deliver a good or service, along with the relationships required to maintain these resources and guide their interactions. For example, the designers of the sixteenth-century "outputting" system that revitalized the European textile industry not only had to imagine a reborn "cottage production" model but also had to develop and distribute the new spindles and wheels that would allow it to operate. Similarly, to take a modern-day example, one visionary in Pennsylvania created a highly successful health care network by conceiving of a "medical mall" in which subscribers could receive "one-stop" health care. He then contacted potential health care providers, oversaw construction of the mall, and brought in the key manager needed to operate this innovative organization.

Thus, the role of network designer may be simply to see, explain, and broaden the awareness of existing avenues for sharing resources creatively. In other instances, the network architect may actually envision the form and function of new network elements and help develop the tools and linkages needed to operate.

THE PROCESS ENGINEERING ROLE—
THE NETWORK CO-OPERATOR

Just as networks do not simply appear without some design activity, they do not simply begin to operate—the specific pieces best suited to the production of a given good or service typically do not come together smoothly or automatically. Someone must take the initiative to hook together the correct elements to generate the appropriate quality and quantity of output and provide the connected elements an appropriate return. This role is similar to that of the process engineer who lays out the flow of resources along the value chain and specifies the operating requirements for each output stage.

However, in the network form, the process engineer's role often extends across traditional organizational boundaries and thus includes the "business" function of achieving agreement on goals, standards, and payments with another firm (or firms). Moreover, these connections among the best-suited network elements may have to be made quickly and inexpensively. That is, if every exchange among elements must be accompanied by a complex contract detailing compliance guarantees, input measures, penalty clauses, and so on, the network's competitive advantages of speed and responsiveness will be lost, and the added cost of each interfirm transaction will damage overall network efficiency. Thus, helping the network organization function across company boundaries responsively and efficiently is the principal focus of the "co-operator" role. In the health care network described above, this role was played jointly by the architect and the medical mall's administrator— managing the new network through a testing period, redesigning referral and accounting processes, and so forth.

THE NURTURING ROLE— THE NETWORK DEVELOPER

Finally, once designed and co-operating, a network must not only be maintained, it must be enhanced. This requires continual attention and nurturing. Indeed, the development of interactive competence among network members is a task very much like that pursued by internal organizational development specialists. Just as these specialists focus on team building and improving communication and coordination processes between an organization's work groups and operating units, the network developer focuses on building interfirm teamwork skills. For example, in the construction industry, "partnering" sessions are held among network members at the beginning of major projects to clarify responsibilities and relationships and to agree on methods of resolving disputes.

The network development role also includes facilitating new member orientation and integration—visiting with firms new to the network to share technical information and insights on how the network operates, including the types of firm behaviors that help or hinder overall network effectiveness. Helping new firms learn to utilize simple contracts or handshake agreements, to think about and volunteer value-adding contributions to partners both upstream and downstream rather than merely responding to their requests, to discipline each other when behavior inimical to the network is detected—all of these help define the network maintenance and development role.

THE NEW ROLES IN PRACTICE

The management roles of architect, co-operator, and developer are found in all types of network organizations. However, the primacy of each role—the extent to which it becomes the crucial, continuing challenge—differs from one type of network to the next. A brief description of these roles at work in stable, dynamic, and internal networks will give both the roles and the different types of networks added meaning.

MANAGING THE STABLE NETWORK

Efficient operation is the key to success in the stable network— the speed and efficiency with which familiar partners interact and adapt as required to meet the demands of each new product or service collaboration. At Nike, for example, conceptualizing its vast outsourcing and distribution network was a demanding task, but most new expansions use variations of past design decisions. Day-to-day success turns on the efficiency with which goods flow from design to production to distribution across country borders to meet highly time-sensitive market demands.

Nike is constantly seeking ways to make the network linkages and flows even less troublesome and more fluid. For example, Nike allows some major distributors to interact directly with the plants producing their orders. In such instances, Nike acts as a product designer and resource broker. This advanced form of co-operating builds on Nike's growing success at creating cooperative, knowledge-building, quality-assuring alliances with an array of upstream and downstream firms.

With new shoe models, Nike's production technicians work with technicians in supplier firms to ensure quality and quantity output requirements, thus sharing technical know-how across the network. Similarly, Nike's marketing experts share insights with their distributor counterparts. Further, Nike is continually working to improve its systems of payment and accounting to ensure mutual benefits without onerous contractual hurdles. Thus, the key organizational task at Nike is to continue to fine-tune network operations—to build more, and more efficient, mechanisms to facilitate product flow through a value chain that Nike does not own, but for which it initiates cooperative activity that is responsive to market demands and that uses market mechanisms to connect and direct its various elements.

At Nike, as in other stable networks, the development role is almost built into the co-operating role. Because most interactions represent return engagements, Nike's earlier operating efforts have been aimed at developing effective linking mechanisms and relationships. Helping a new supplier build the competence to produce for Nike and others is not just a technical task, it is a relationship-building task as well. Further, Nike's willingness to trust and share knowledge with upstream and downstream firms tends to be reciprocated, laying the foundation for creative new operating experiments and productive future linkages.

MANAGING THE DYNAMIC NETWORK

In a dynamic network, the architect's role is most likely to be the key to long-term success. The ability to envision not only the design of new products and services but also the rich array of potential partners that might be employed in their production dominates this type of network. At such firms as Dell (personal computers), Novell (computer software), and Galoob (toys and novelties), upstream and/or downstream partners are constantly changing to meet the demands of new products or services, utilize available capacity, stimulate or create new patterns of cooperation, and so on. Moreover, all of each firm's partners have many other partners of their own, each turning from one to another to fill its needs in a constantly shifting business environment. Leading firms in such networks spend much of their time locating potential new partners, expanding the network to ensure even greater responsiveness.

In service industries a similar dynamism is apparent, with firms at every point along the value chain taking part in the network design role. For example, a motion picture sound-editing studio needs a global network of production firms to keep its expensive assets—people and equipment—fully utilized. So too does a firm providing advanced forms of computer animation, such as Industrial Light and Magic. Indeed, much of the motion picture industry reflects characteristics of a giant, global dynamic network, one in which the search for new players and richer interactive potential is a constant challenge. In this form of network, the various elements along the value chain are fully aware of their interdependencies and thus are motivated not only to connect quickly and easily but also to ensure that their inputs are of the highest possible quality. In other service industries as well, such as publishing and consulting, the contributions of firms all along the value chain are highly visible, as creative competitors are always waiting in the wings.

MANAGING THE INTERNAL NETWORK

In the internal network, the crucial management role is development—maintaining and enhancing the conditions under which commonly owned elements can interact through market forces instead of through constant appeals to managers higher in the hierarchy. At ABB, for example, the initial organizational design created three interactive components: (1) domestically focused national companies, (2) profit-center plants producing for both domestic and international distribution, and (3) globally focused business area teams placing plant output in markets around the world. All of these organizational components interact in response to market forces, and they exchange goods and services at market prices. Although such a design has clear operating routines, it is highly vulnerable to corporate interference. Periodic commands from corporate headquarters to move resources at other than market price, for example, can damage internal guidance mechanisms, since profit performance is no longer a meaningful measure once market prices have been distorted or replaced.

Unfortunately, many internal networks have not drawn continuing developmental attention. Members at all levels do not get the assistance they need to understand the "economy" they are charged with operating. Further, they may be forced to deal with intentional or inadvertent intervention by higher-level managers. Therefore, learning how to maintain the integrity of the market inside an internal network may still be one of modern management's most consuming challenges.

THE SPHERICAL ORGANIZATION

Successful network organizations often reveal their inspired design simplicity, creative connection mechanisms and operating approaches, and dedicated development efforts. The network roles of architect, co-operator, and developer are natural extensions across firms of well-understood, though not always effectively discharged, internal management functions. Thus, with sufficient motivation, managers can learn and practice these roles in a wide variety of emerging network settings. For most network managers, barriers to the effective performance of these roles are likely to be more ideological than intellectual, a phenomenon we will explore in the next chapter.

However, one set of new management requirements increasingly apparent in network organizations presents both an intellectual and a philosophical hurdle for many managers. These demands involve how a given firm must be designed and managed internally in order to meet its external network opportunities and obligations. In this arena, a new metaphor—a new way of envisioning the internal operation of a particular network member—may be essential.

For example, in discussing the shift from large centrally controlled firms to disaggregated, market-guided networks, we borrowed Ackoff's concept of corporate perestroika—the breakup of centrally planned economies and their movement toward collections of market-driven companies. Similarly, at the level of a firm in a network organization, an equally powerful metaphor is needed, one that replaces that of the organization as pyramid. Such a metaphor is the rotating sphere (see Figure 8–1).

FROM FIXED TO ROTATING RESOURCES

The usual organization chart portrays rows of offices in a pyramid, from the CEO through division and department heads, down to the rank-and-file employee. Its shape suggests a stable, unified focus on the environment—problems enter the hierarchy and solutions leave it. In contrast, we know that the essence of network effectiveness is flexible, rapid response—the ability to quickly arrange and rearrange resources to meet the changing, customized needs of upstream and downstream partners, and ultimately those of customers. To meet this need, we must repackage the pyramid's resources, figuratively and almost literally, into a rotatable sphere.

Imagine the resources of a firm arrayed around the exterior of a sphere, as shown in Figure 8–1. Now imagine that the sphere rotates upon request, to bring the required resources into contact with particular requests from partners at other points along the value chain, from peers occupying the same value-chain position, from customers, or from potential partners outside the activated network. Thus, an interaction can begin from any angle: wherever a request touches the sphere, the initiator's needs are

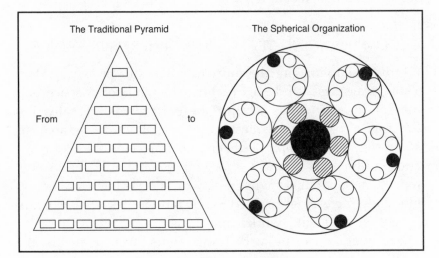

Figure 8–1 The Firm of the Future

processed, and signals are sent to rotate the sphere to bring the necessary resources into alignment with the request's initiator.

This metaphor is descriptive of the way a medical clinic might respond to a patient's needs, with the initial diagnosis bringing in an array of specialized expertise in response. It is, in fact, how the health care providers function in the "medical mall" network described earlier. Wherever a client enters the system, it adjusts to meet his or her needs quickly and effectively. It is also descriptive of the way a highly service-oriented department store, such as Nordstrom's, operates. A customer entering at any door is met by the first available salesperson, who then directs, perhaps even escorts, the customer to the appropriate department and "introduces" him or her to another salesperson.

Increasingly, customers are co-participating in the design of desired products (e.g., home design), and their requests to highly networked firms are often received directly by self-managed teams of skilled personnel who possess the abilities needed to deliver the goods or services or can direct the customer to the appropriate provider. Such firms, coupled with their just-in-time linked-up network partners, are "virtual" organizations, capable, once triggered, of achieving operating substance almost instantly .

SELF-MANAGING TEAMS—THE SPHERE'S BEARINGS

It is difficult to imagine the entire resources of a firm arrayed on a spherical surface. Indeed, the sphere has an interior space, and the spherical firm has work to be performed internally. For example, a customer's request is sent to a laboratory for analysis and design testing, a part is taken into a machine shop for alteration, a film is taken into a studio for sound editing, and so on. Indeed, much of the activity in network firms of any size occurs internally, increasingly carried out by individuals who are members of self-managing work teams.

The operation of network firms favors, even demands, the creation and use of self-managing teams to facilitate both responsiveness and the efficient utilization of resources. The members of self-managing teams are cross-trained to provide extensive backup for all the skills required in the team's domain, and most members can provide a broad array of these skills effectively. Moreover, in the self-managing team, extensive training builds the team's capacity to guide its own resources—to plan, schedule, and coordinate activities within the team, and across teams as needed, to meet a particular product or service request.

Imagine inside a spherical network firm, then, a collection of smaller, spherically shaped bearings, each a self-managing work team. Further, each of these team bearings is itself made up of a collection of individuals who are generalists. Indeed, the ability of the spherical firm to rotate smoothly is dependent on the extent to which its internal mechanisms—teams and individuals—are themselves friction-free and flexible. If self-managing teams are fully rotatable, all of the firm's "internal" resources can be quickly rotated to the surface—to become temporary leaders of interactions with other network members or with groups outside the network.

In an increasing number of network firms, self-managing teams are being drawn off the shop floor, or out of offices or labs, and brought into direct contact with customers or suppliers. Alternatively, a single member of the team may make a "surface" contact before rotating the remainder of a team into position to meet a particular request. Having studied a number of self-managing teams in Italian network organizations, Vincenzo Perrone has concluded that network firms can be no more flexible and effective externally than they are internally—the quality of their external relationships and service is determined by their ability to arrange and manage their internal resources.[2] The firm that relies on traditional internal hierarchical arrangements and mechanisms can engage in only limited external linkages, and can bring only a few resources to bear on any given request. Conversely, the firm that develops highly facilitative internal arrangements, such as self-managing teams, can multiply and enrich its external linkages.

CONTINUOUS TRAINING AND DEVELOPMENT

Clearly, the lubricant for these team bearings and for the spherical firm itself is knowledge and skills gained through continuous training and development. The more technical, business, and self-governance skills possessed by team members individually and by the team collectively, the more resources a network firm can bring to bear on any request and the quicker those resources can be focused.[3]

TCG: A SPHERICAL NETWORK[4]

The metaphor of the spherical firm, rotating freely on its self-managed team bearing, provides a graphic image of the firm of the future. When several such firms are hooked together in a voluntary, cooperative network, the makings of a spherical organization are at hand. One group of firms that illustrates the spherical network organization in operation is Technical and Computer Graphics (TCG). Located in Sydney, TCG is a group of small companies that, by practicing very sophisticated leadership and self-management, has become the largest privately owned computer services business in Australia. Starting as a small computer service operation of four people in 1971, TCG has grown to become a highly interactive network of twenty-four companies with annual revenues of approximately $50 million and a staff of about two hundred. TCG is now considered to be one of Australia's most significant innovators in portable data terminals, computer graphics, simulators, bar-coding systems, electronic data interchange, electronic identification tags, and other applications of information and communications technology.

Within TCG, new product development—and hence network expansion—is called "triangulation," meaning that it involves a three-cornered partnership among a TCG firm, a similar technology-based firm outside TCG, and a major customer. The triangular product development process typically involves five key steps.

STEP 1: IDENTIFY THE MARKET NICHE

All twenty-four TCG member firms constantly search for new product or service opportunities in data capturing, electronic data interchange, computing, and other specialized applications. Thus, each TCG network firm is a "rotatable bearing" connected to the marketplace. It is TCG that researches an application and develops a strategy for its development. When a particular application appears to have concrete potential, the initiating TCG firm becomes the project's leader.

STEP 2: FIND A DEVELOPMENT PARTNER

The leader firm then seeks a non-TCG company with complementary skills, markets, or technologies to be a partner in the development of the application. The partner firm, called a "joint venturer," brings with it access to new markets or prospects for collaboration. The TCG firm, in turn, is attractive to the joint venturer because it provides access to TCG companies' expertise through its leadership role. With each of its member firms playing the role of leader in other ventures, the total network is always developing and expanding.

STEP 3: LOCATE A MAJOR CUSTOMER

TCG scans the world for likely customers for the emerging product. It seeks one of these to come into a partnership arrangement as the "principal" customer, whose large initial order wins it contractual rights (e.g., preferential supply, best price, and/or marketing rights in its domain) that extend beyond those of other customers. Typically, the principal customer is not offered equity participation; this is reserved for the joint venturer, which has its eye on future developments in fields outside the domain of the principal customer. Thus, the principal customer's order provides the cash needed to pursue the venture.

STEP 4: INVOLVE OTHER TCG FIRMS

In addition to its linkages with the joint venturer and principal customer, the leader firm must rotate inward to bring appropriate TCG network firms into the product development process. From this point on, the leader firm is the gateway through which information and resources flow into and out of the network.

STEP 5: EXTEND THE TRIANGLE IN NEW DIRECTIONS

As product development proceeds, the joint venturers typically will look for further business opportunities. This takes each of the partners in the triangle in new directions. TCG, in particular, seeks to link the development to others it has in the pipeline, generating further ideas and joint ventures that can, in turn, be triangulated with new principal customers. In this way, the TCG spherical network expands and renews itself across its entire surface. (For a description of the ten principles that govern TCG's activities, see Table 8–1.)

Unleashing the Power of a Spherical Network

We have indicated how network organizations, and the spherical design of each of their elements (firms), flow naturally from the demanding competitive environments most companies are facing—environments that are demanding both efficiency and customized responsiveness at an ever faster pace.

However, there are also internal forces driving the network form. Indeed, once created, networks and their elements tend to perpetuate and enhance the forces that spawned them. That is, the ability of the network form to adapt creatively generates the opportunity for more adaptation. It not only speeds the flow of innovative products and services, it also speeds the adoption of new technologies and new ways of arranging resources to operate them, thus creating richer and richer networks.

Table 8–1
HOW TCG GOVERNS ITS SPHERICAL ORGANIZATION

1. *Mutual Independence*
   The TCG network consists of independent firms whose relations are governed by bilateral commercial contracts. It is open to new entrants who are prepared to abide by the rules. There is no internal hierarchy.

2. *Mutual Preference*
   Member firms give preference to each other in the letting of contracts. Contracts may be made outside the group, against a competitive bid from a member firm, when circumstances warrant (e.g., work overload or a signal to the member firm that it has to lift its game).

3. *Mutual Noncompetition*
   Member firms do not compete head-to-head with each other. Such self-denial helps to establish trust among member firms.

4. *Mutual Nonexploitation*
   Member firms do not seek to make profits from transactions among themselves.

5. *Flexibility and Business Autonomy*
   The flexibility of the network as a whole derives from the capacity of member firms to respond to opportunities as they see fit. They do not need to ask for group approval to enter into any transation or new line of business, provided the proposed innovation does not breach any rules.

6. *Network Democracy*
   There is no overall network owner. Nor is there any central committee or other formal governance structure. However, member firms can hold equity in each other as well as in third-party joint venturers.

7. *Expulsion*
   A firm may be expelled from the network if it willfully disobeys the rules. Expulsion can be effected simply by severing all commercial ties with the miscreant member.

8. *Subcontracting*
   There are no "subcontractor-only" firms within the TCG group. Each member firm has access to the open market, and indeed is expected to bring in work from outside.

9. *Entry*
   New members are welcome to join the network but are not to draw financial resources from the group. New members must obtain capital from banks rather than through equity from other member firms. It is membership in the network that serves as collateral for the bank loan.

10. *Exit*
    The network places no impediments in the way of a departing firm. However, there is no market for shares held in TCG member firms; hence, departure arrangements have to be negotiated on a case-by-case basis.

Source: Adapted from John Mathews, *TCG: Sustainable Economic Organisation Through Networking* (Kensington, Australia: Industrial Relations Research Centre, The University of New South Wales, 1992), pages 25–27.

In fact, the internal push for increased network quality and capacity can be seen at every level. This push comes from self-managed teams inside the network firm, from the network firm outward toward the broader set of its current and potential partners, and from the network organization itself—forward toward an ever-broadening array of customers, backward toward a growing population of suppliers, and outward toward related networks in the global economy.

THE PUSH FROM A SELF-MANAGING TEAM

Once created, an empowered work team with constantly growing business and technical knowledge gains a momentum of its own; it tends to outgrow its existing set of responsibilities and assignments. It anticipates and responds quickly to new demands, growing in competence with each success. Ultimately, it pushes the firm to seek new opportunities to utilize its developing competence—to reward it for its continued growth.[5]

The motivation and competence of self-managing teams to grow beyond their existing operations has been documented in a variety of plants and offices. Unfortunately, in many instances, firms that have invested in self-managing work teams have been either unable or unwilling to continue to provide their teams with challenging assignments once needed output has been achieved.

However, the network firm, with its propensity toward creating linkages with other firms to serve an increasing client base, has a greater potential for utilizing the growing capabilities of self-managing teams. For example, the network firm, as described above, can rotate a team into direct contact with a new customer. At Xerox Corporation, self-managing teams are responsible for products all the way from the laboratory to the customer. Some, such as logistics and distribution services groups, have been turned into full-fledged business units, selling services both inside and outside the firm.

Innovative companies such as the 3M Corporation are adept at spinning off internally generated product "partnerships" in which the firm retains a partial financial stake but the developing team runs as an independent business. Most teams in network firms do not become business units as such. However, opportunities for growth and development are usually greater than in non-network firms. Many teams do have the opportunity to use their resources across firm boundaries from time to time, and most develop the ability to measure and evaluate the value they add to the firm's output. In fact, carefully measuring the value the team adds is a key part of the team's "business" education and development, and is the basis both for performance-based reward systems and for marketing the team's services outside the firm.

In sum, network firms invest in self-management for their work teams not to make the team members happy but to make them more productive and adaptive. In turn, teams push the network firm to expand its own vision—to build broader linkages and to find more partners, so that the team's growing capabilities can be utilized and rewarded.

THE PUSH FROM THE
NETWORK FIRM

The network firm, pushed from the inside by its own members, expands the network quantitatively or qualitatively each time it provides a high-quality service to a new partner. Each time a network firm is successfully linked upstream or downstream, the potential for a future interaction is enhanced. That is, once firms find that networking works, they tend to develop greater confidence in the form. With greater confidence, they use the form more and this, in turn, develops their competence in making the form work even more effectively.

Indeed, the very act of using the network makes it easier for the network to expand. Greater use creates demand for more network firms, and each additional element in the network creates both the potential for and the likelihood of more use. For example, as a downstream firm sees more potential suppliers available, it is less likely to invest in its own vertical integration. As the network expands, barriers to downstream entry are lowered, and new "designer" firms can expand the customer base for the entire network.

Similarly, upstream entrants may also expand network potential by bringing new technology to the production of parts and components, thus allowing new designs to emerge. For example, some years ago Boeing, which had a reputation for doing everything in-house, began experimenting with linkages to outside suppliers and even alliances with outside designers. By following practices used extensively by its European and other competitors, Boeing increased the size and effectiveness of the network available to all competitors, and more use begat more use. In fact, Boeing's 777 involved extensive outsourcing and collaboration at all stages of development. Currently, McDonnell-Douglas is attempting to create a "super jumbo" airplane by relying heavily on a network organization—collaborating with suppliers at every point along the value chain.

THE NETWORK ORGANIZATION'S PUSH ON THE INDUSTRY AND ECONOMY

Truly effective networks, by combining customized responsiveness and efficiency, may push their own industries to higher levels of performance. Recent research indicates that industries with greater variation in firm strategy and behavior tend to outperform their more homogeneous counterparts.[6] Networks, both on their own and as a competitive spur to non-network firms, appear to produce just such variety.

While direct performance comparisons between "high-network" and "low-network" industries have not yet been fully explored, it does seem clear that the network form has improved performance in many industries, including motion pictures, publishing, telecommunications, health care, and so on. Clearly, the network organization has stimulated economic development in many parts of the world, particularly where supplier firms in underdeveloped countries serve large global corporations. For example, Korea entered the U.S.

automobile market with a car designed, manufactured, and distributed using many features of the network form. The electronics industries of Taiwan, Hong Kong, and Singapore owe much of their energy to the existence of global networks for designing, producing, and distributing consumer electronics products.

Of course, there are costs associated with the network form. Lowered barriers to entry can create oversupply and may drive profit margins to low levels. Nevertheless, network experience builds technical and business competence, and it creates new markets at the same time as it creates new supply.

POINTS OF FRICTION IN THE SPHERICAL ORGANIZATION

The network form, like the organizational forms that preceded it, has demanded that managers learn different roles and new ways of thinking about organizing. Again, like earlier forms, it emerged in response to the competitive conditions of the time, but it has developed its own internal pressure for broader and broader use. Each network firm builds greater strength and creativity internally as it learns to interact more effectively and vice versa. Moreover, as a given network firm builds its competence, it pushes its partners to build theirs. Finally, the network as a whole is both the product of its environment and the creator of a new environment, one that will place more demands on the network but also provide it with more opportunity. The linked network firms need managers who understand the relationships among firms and can capitalize on them.

Networks pushed along by their own momentum are likely to be slowed down only by a major shift in the external environment or, even more likely, by resistance on the part of managers who do not find the network and its new managerial roles compatible with their own philosophies of management. As has been the case with prior organizational forms, the principal barrier to the effective application and continued operation of the network form is the failure of managers to understand and accept a philosophy of management that facilitates rather than inhibits this type of organizational approach. In Chapter 9, we will explore a new philosophy of management that is emerging in leading-edge organizations and consider its implications for these firms and for management in general.

CHAPTER 9

A NEW MANAGERIAL PHILOSOPHY:

The Human Investment Model

The network organization, especially in its more advanced spherical form, represents a significant departure from previous organizational forms. Its demand for new roles and relationships is challenging to today's managers. The challenges reflect two major barriers that managers must overcome in order to be able to build and operate effective networks. The first barrier is essentially an intellectual one. While the core logic of the network form can be derived from its organizational predecessors, the broader concept of multifirm interactions having both market and organizational properties may be difficult to grasp.

The second barrier is attitudinal. Even if managers understand the network form's operating logic, they may resist its requirements because these are in direct conflict with some managers' deeply held beliefs about people and how they should be managed. Nevertheless, given past experience, it seems reasonable to expect that many managers will respond positively to the challenges of managing a network organization. They will not only operate networks with increasing understanding, they will creatively modify and develop them. Moreover, managers will articulate and internalize a new managerial philosophy that will reflect the richness of the network form and reinforce its operating logic.

In this chapter, we will identify the forces pushing managers toward a new philosophy of management. We will then describe this philosophy, which we call the human investment model.[1] Finally, we will illustrate the new philosophy in practice, showing in particular how it is pushing managers to make investments in trust building at the individual, team, firm, and network levels.

FORCES SHAPING THE NEW MANAGERIAL PHILOSOPHY

A new managerial philosophy has begun to appear and is rapidly evolving in many of our most successful companies. This new philosophy is being shaped by three interrelated forces: (1) ideological—the felt need within the management profession to rationalize and explain new roles and relationships in the modern organization; (2) societal—the pressure to respond to changing societal values, ideals, and expectations; and (3) technical—the clear requirement for new managerial behaviors dictated by the operating requirements of an organizational form.

IDEOLOGICAL FORCES

In every period, managers feel pressure to rationalize and articulate how, why, and by what right they manage organizations and their members. That is, they feel the need to explain, both to others and to themselves, their relationships with peers, subordinates, customers, suppliers, and so on—including where and by whom decisions will be made and authority exercised. In the early twentieth century, for example, owner-managers gave way to professional managers with the emergence of large-scale functional organizations. This new class of managers felt the need to develop explanations that rationalized expertise- rather than ownership-based authority. In a later period, corporate managers in divisional firms felt the need to justify their use of stockholder funds to support diversification strategies.

In the current period, managers in network organizations recognize the need to rationalize this form's broad demands for changes in management practices. For example, managers need to explain how and why traditional hierarchical controls are being supplanted by market mechanisms. Increasingly, they need to explain the growing necessity to disperse decision-making authority throughout the organization and beyond its current boundaries.

SOCIETAL FORCES

Along with the need to rationalize and explain the managerial approach required by the network organization, managers feel a pressure to relate their managerial practices to changes in values occurring in the broader society. This is more than just a logical exercise. Managers themselves are participants in the broader process of change. Thus, their work organizations and their role within them cannot be greatly out of line with society's expectations and values. Again, the relationship between managerial philosophies and changing social values is evident in earlier transitional periods. For example, the human relations philosophy of management not only explained and justified managers' roles in large functional organizations, it also captured many of the values of the reform movements of the early twentieth century—among which were those aimed at improving the working conditions of women and children. Similarly, the human resources philosophy emerged in the late 1950s and 1960s alongside the beginnings of the civil rights movement. Not surprisingly, this philosophy's emphasis on broad employee participation in important work decisions paralleled the pressure for broadened participation in civic and economic affairs by minority group members.

In the current transition, both the network organization and the broader society are responding to heightened demands for opportunities and advancement by all members of society. Managers feel the need to make certain that their organizations not only demand high levels of performance from a diverse work force, but also provide the rewards such performance justifies, including enhanced career options both within the firm and throughout employees' working lives.

TECHNICAL FORCES

In addition to the felt need to provide a consistent explanation of managerial behaviors that reflect societal values, managers feel a practical need to respond to the many specific demands of their organizations. For example, the network organization simply will not operate if managers attempt to exercise direct personal control and/or tight, complex, and expensive legal control over supplier relationships. Even though some managers may not have fully rationalized the position and responsibilities of their firm and those of their customers and suppliers along the value chain, they are still confronted by the technical requirement to create efficient, low-cost interaction mechanisms.

Similar demands were made by new organizational forms in earlier periods.[2] For example, whether or not managers had fully adopted the human relations philosophy, the need for a loyal and cooperative work force, as opposed to a rebellious and transient one, was obvious in the large functional organizations. Similarly, even managers who were not philosophically prepared to advocate decision-making autonomy were forced by the pace and volume of decision-making demands in divisional and matrix organizations to grant some broadened decision-making authority. In the network organization, both internal and external demands push managerial behavior along at a faster pace than many managers' own beliefs would advocate. When this occurs, changes in attitudes and philosophies may well follow new required behaviors rather than precede them.

In sum, managerial philosophies today are being shaped by ideological, societal, and technical demands in modern organizations and the surrounding society. These forces are producing a new philosophy of management, one that is and will continue to develop along an identifiable pathway.

THE HUMAN INVESTMENT PHILOSOPHY: ASSUMPTIONS, POLICIES, AND EXPECTATIONS

The shape of the new philosophy of management has been emerging over the last ten years or so. It has evolved in response to dramatic changes that have reshaped the world of business, brought major social trends into sharper focus, and placed new and heavy demands on the profession of management. However, while portions of the new philosophy are clearly visible in managers' statements and practices in some leading firms, its full shape and implications have not been articulated. Nevertheless, because the current evolutionary process resembles those of the past, we can identify and extend most of the new philosophy's essential features. That is, just as each new organizational form builds on its predecessors, incorporating some features, adapting others, and creating new mechanisms to respond to environmental demands, managerial philosophies also evolve one from another. Thus, the human resources philosophy adopted, modified, and expanded significantly many of the assumptions, policies, and expectations of the human relations model. In turn, the human investment model is adapting and extending the assumptions, policy prescriptions, and expectations of the human resources model. In the following sections, we will explore the adaptations being made in each of these areas, comparing the new model's assumptions with those of earlier philosophies.

ASSUMPTIONS ABOUT PEOPLE

As previously illustrated in Table 2–1, and as shown in Table 9–1 below, managerial philosophies are built on a core set of assumptions about people, particularly their capabilities and trustworthiness. For example, with regard to *capability*, the human relations model viewed most organizational members not only as capable of carrying out orders but also as having the ability to contribute ideas and suggestions to improve their own tasks and procedures. The human resources model expanded this view, envisioning most organization members as having an untapped capacity to contribute to the making of important decisions and to exercise creative self-direction and control. The emerging human investment philosophy focuses not so much on current abilities as on the potential of organization members to develop broad technical and self-governance skills, that is, the capability to grow new competencies to meet tomorrow's needs. The belief in essentially unlimited human potential encourages

Table 9–1
THE HUMAN INVESTMENT PHILOSOPHY

Assumptions:

1. Most people not only want to contribute and have untapped capabilities. They also have the potential to continually develop their technical skills, their self-governance competency, and their understanding of business issues.
2. Most people, both inside the network firm and across current and future partner firms, are trustworthy as well as trusting in their relationships. They can and will develop broad interpersonal and interorganizational communications skills with education and encouragement.

Policies:

1. The manager's basic task is to prepare the organization's human and technical resources to respond effectively and efficiently to current and future demands within the organization's scope of operation.
2. The manager must make both current and long-term investments in technical skills upgrading as well as general business and self-management knowledge for every organizational member.
3. The manager must give individual employees and self-managing teams every opportunity to practice new skills and exercise new knowledge; the manager must view human capabilities as a venture capitalist, investing in employees' long-term growth and developing competence.
4. Managers must be prepared to make investments in both technical and governance skills across organizational units within other network member firms.

Expectations:

1. Investments in human capabilities, including self-governance competence, builds adaptive capacity and creates a learning organization.
2. The more competent the manager's own organization, the more facile and effective are the network linkages it can make.

Adapted from Raymond E. Miles and W.E. Douglas Creed, "Organizational Forms and Managerial Philosophies," Working Paper, Haas School of Business, University of California, Berkeley, 1994.

continuous investment in the company's human assets as the means of maintaining organizational effectiveness in a constantly changing environment.

Similarly, in terms of *trustworthiness,* the human relations philosophy challenged the prevailing traditional view that most people are inherently lazy and uncooperative. Indeed, it predicted that workers would demonstrate loyalty and commitment in return for humane treatment and the opportunity to gain recognition and approval. The human resources philosophy expanded this view, expecting that most organization members would work responsibly to achieve jointly set goals. The human investment model goes beyond these assumptions, attributing trustworthiness not only to members of the immediate firm but to upstream and downstream partners across the broader network as well. Again, the belief that people inside and outside the network firm will meet expectations and respond creatively implies that managers can afford to make investments and take risks in the interest of continuing organizational adaptation and improvement.

While the shape of the human investment model and its contrasts to earlier philosophies are easily illustrated in terms of its assumptions about capability and trustworthiness, the model's implications for managerial policy and practice are also crucial for a full understanding of this philosophy.

IMPLICATIONS FOR MANAGEMENT POLICIES AND PRACTICES

Like its predecessor philosophies, the human investment approach to management has important implications for leadership, job design, planning and control systems, individual and team development programs, and the design of reward systems.

Under the human investment philosophy, managers' primary *leadership* role is to create development-based, self-governing partnerships. The intent is to create the opportunity and capacity for individuals and work teams to exercise broad market-directed self-governance. Self-governance can only occur as a result of heavy investment in technical, business, and leadership skills. Such skills are visible within work teams in many advanced organizations, teams capable of interacting directly with customers, suppliers, investors, and so on. These teams are knowledgeable not only about products and processes but also about costs, pricing, and the capital requirements of their product group. Carried to its limits, the human investment model sees leadership not as a superior-subordinate relationship but as a shared responsibility among peers or colleagues.

The leadership implications of the human investment philosophy can be more fully appreciated by noting the evolution of leadership concepts and prescriptions across previous managerial philosophies. The leadership role of owner-managers sharing the traditional philosophy was to inspire and control, and the mechanism was direct supervision. The leadership role under the human relations model was to support and persuade. Here the mechanism was limited participation in matters of mostly routine importance. The leadership role under the human resources model was to facilitate and fully utilize member resources, and the mechanisms were joint goal setting and broad participation in important work issues.

Note that the leadership objectives under the human investment model are to broaden the responsibilities of all organization members to include not only the demands of the production process but business and governance responsibilities as well. Moreover, it is not the manager's job to determine the skills necessary to exercise these responsibilities. It is the manager's job only to invest in the opportunity for members to develop those skills.

In the area of *job design*, the human investment philosophy once again seeks to create the ability of all members to become partners in the design of their contributions—to develop their capability to respond broadly to changing market needs and to adapt their activities to complement those of other organization members. Here, also, the implications of the model may best be seen in comparison with the job design implications of previous philosophies.

Recall that the traditional model advocated the creation of specialized tasks of narrow scope that could be quickly learned and accomplished following standard procedures and methods. The human relations model, seeking to respond to member needs for less boring work, advocated job enlargement—increasing the range of specialized tasks among which an individual might rotate. The human resources model advocated job enrichment, vertically loading jobs by adding responsibility for quality, scheduling, and so forth.

The human investment model seeks to create empowered jobs—jobs that charge members with meeting broad responsibilities by whatever means are appropriate. The empowered hotel desk clerk does whatever is required to make a valued customer satisfied. The empowered research and development team exercises broad judgment and controls the resources needed to carry projects through to completion.

Under the human investment model, *planning and control* information is routed directly to those who need it to make decisions. With such information, and with clear criteria based on a shared understanding of business needs, individuals and teams exercise self-control in the service of the organization.

Information in a traditional system is closely held by the owner-manager and is shared in the form of commands and instructions. Control is exercised through direct observation. Under the human relations model, managers determined the work and business information to be shared with subordinates and provided mechanisms for limited feedback, such as suggestion systems and periodic department meetings. Control was exercised through supervision and the collection of progress reports and cost data. Under the human resources model, managers were expected to share information as required for the discussion and setting of joint goals. Control was exercised through supervision, schedule and budget data, and review sessions focused on achievements related to jointly set goals.

The human investment model expects individuals and teams to develop the capacity to control their own activities and resources in a manner that adds high value to organizational output. In effect, the effort is to create a collegial structure in which participants exchange relevant planning and control information while individually and collectively meeting the organization's needs.

By this point, it should be clear that the human investment model is aimed at *continuous development*. However, the implications of the model go beyond simply advocating an increase in the quantity of developmental activities and investments. Indeed, perhaps the key feature of development under this philosophy is the expectation of shared responsibility.

Under the traditional model, development objectives were limited to skill-training requirements for the worker's immediate job. The human relations model offered training in a series of related tasks and, for selected employees, training opportunities that might lead to advancement to staff or supervisory positions. Under the human resources philosophy, development goals were expanded to include a much broader range of job skills and educational opportunities, providing they could be justified in terms of current and future organizational needs. Note that while development scope and objectives expand as managerial philosophies evolve over time, control and responsibility for the development process shifts only minimally. Management decides what training and development needs exist, and either decides who will take part or allows members to participate in making those decisions.

In the human investment philosophy, a key differentiating factor is that development investments need not be justified in terms of specific current or future organizational needs. Indeed, the human investment philosophy explicitly recognizes that in today's fast-paced world, future skills and knowledge requirements are seldom fully predictable. Equally if not more important, the human investment philosophy recognizes that organizational members must be partners in the development process. In the flexible organization of tomorrow, all members must accept major responsibility for their own careers—their progress in the current organization and their movement among organizations to find outlets for their growing skills and abilities. No management can effectively plan the careers of an increasingly diverse and competent work force with its own shifting needs and opportunities. Management can only work with organization members to provide an expanding set of training and educational opportunities, financed by the company's own investments as well as those of its members.

The human investment model does not advocate a particular type of *reward system*. Instead, it anticipates that all organization members will have knowledge and responsibilities with bottom-line implications. Thus, all members may well be involved in companywide reward schemes based on bottom-line performance. More directly, the human investment model provides the opportunity for work teams to become nearly autonomous sub-contractors—for individual members to invest in and manage projects they have helped to create, and for organizations as a whole to share their gains with upstream and downstream partners. Indeed, the whole thrust of the human investment model is to bring all aspects of the firm and its internal and external constituents into direct contact with the market forces shaping their destiny, and to enable all members to experience success or failure based on their own skills and efforts.

Each of the previous philosophies implies some form of output- or cost-based reward sharing. The key difference of the human investment philosophy is the recognition that no reward system is complete and viable unless all participants have the skills, information, and responsibilities needed to be full partners in both the creation of outcomes and the sharing of rewards.

EXPECTATIONS

The third dimension of all managerial philosophies is a set of expectations. If people in the organization are as the model assumes and the policies advocated by the philosophy are followed, certain consequences will follow.

The expectations of the traditional model were not high. Workers with little competence, closely supervised to prevent them from soldiering on the job, were expected to meet minimal standards. The human relations model was still patronizing, but expectations were higher. Despite their limited capabilities, people could be expected to cooperate and do their best if their need for humane treatment, recognition, and involvement were satisfied. The human resources model called for both high expectations and the freedom to fail. It argued that people's skills and abilities were typically undervalued. By involving them in important decisions and allowing broad self-direction, managers and employees would directly add major value to the firm's output.

The human investment model goes well beyond its predecessors in terms of expectations. It assumes that organization members have the potential to be fully self-managing partners in the enterprise, not only by helping to meet organizational objectives but also by being directly involved in generating new business—that is, acting like entrepreneurs. The human resources model viewed the manager as the principal entrepreneur, investing underutilized human talent to meet the firm's objectives. The human investment model views the manager as a venture capitalist, helping the many entrepreneurs within the firm to gain maximum advantage from their own business and production creativity. Just as venture capitalists seek an equity stake in an enterprise capable of major success, a firm following the human investment model seeks a stake in numerous internal enterprises. It has high expectations of an organization in which everyone is a businessperson.

THE MODEL IN ACTION: INVESTING IN INDIVIDUALS, TEAMS, FIRMS, AND NETWORKS

True to its name, the new philosophy described here emphasizes investment as the key determinant of organizational success—continual investment to upgrade both the firm's human assets and its ability to use them creatively. Moreover, the model is distinguished not only by the volume of investment it advocates, but also by the scope and focus of that investment. As noted, the key assumption of the human investment model is that capability is widely distributed, as is the capacity to develop broad technical, business, and self-governance skills. A further assumption is that these skills will only flourish in an atmosphere of mutual trust and respect—the sort of trust and respect accorded business partners or professional colleagues. Most important, the model recognizes that competencies and trust must be built—they do not appear by pronouncement. Thus, the model anticipates specific management actions that build trust and competence at every level. In the following sections, we will explore some of the specific investment actions implied by the model.

INVESTING IN CAPABILITIES AND TRUST AT THE INDIVIDUAL LEVEL

At the individual level, the approach implied by the human investment model is akin to that common among the professions and the highest levels of skilled artisans. In such groups, (1) capability and trust investments cover broad educational opportunities to develop intellectual muscle and the ability to learn; (2) training and education focus on specific skills and know-how; and (3) apprenticeship relationships provide role models, insights, and an appreciation for the values and expectations of the occupation.

The apprentice emerges from a long process of investment to become the skilled journeyman, a professional who guides his or her own behavior and is responsible for adding value in every work setting in which he or she is involved. We trust professionals to act out the values of their profession, giving us a full return on our investment. Just as competence is built through education and training, trust is built by trusting—by treating the apprentice from the beginning as a colleague, and taking the risk that our trust will be returned. Clearly, the apprentice who falters will be corrected but then trusted again. At the individual level, as at all levels, managers unwilling to take the risk of trusting will not be likely to gain a full return on their investment in skills and abilities.

At Lincoln Electric,[3] individual responsibility and self-management is tied to the company's famous incentive pay system, which annually rewards the typical Lincoln employee with a salary and bonus nearly twice that of workers in similar classifications at other firms. The success of the pay system depends on a continuous investment of management and employee time and effort. Improvements in work processes are constantly being made at Lincoln, some through employee initiative and some through management insights and technical breakthroughs. Each of these requires a reexamination of the standards against which each self-managing employee or work team is evaluated for pay purposes. As such, each change represents an opportunity to build trust or destroy it. It is a testimony to management's commitment to James F. Lincoln's original philosophy,[4] and its diligence in working to ensure that employees perform responsibly in pursuit of their own and the firm's best interests, that the incentive pay system is moving into its tenth decade.

INVESTING IN CAPABILITIES AND TRUST AT THE TEAM LEVEL

In terms of human capital investment, team building probably reaches its zenith in the extended process of creating self-managing work teams in both plants and offices. In these settings, team builders routinely invest heavily in team skill development, particularly the cross-training needed to develop team flexibility and an understanding of the total production and business process. Prior to technical skill training, team builders often put newly formed teams through a variety of exercises to build awareness of common responsibilities and to foster the skills needed for self-governance, including the ability to manage interteam relations. In the most advanced applications, investments in self-governance skills, along with job process skills, are viewed as a continuous process with corresponding continuous returns.

At Chaparral Steel, a commitment has been made to invest up to 30 percent of the time of all organization members in training and education.[5] Building an entire work force of "shop-floor metallurgists," who understand not only how to make steel but how to make money, is an example of the emerging human investment philosophy.

Whether in the office or in the plant, investments in team self-governance skills based on business knowledge is growing among U.S. companies. The expectation is that an employee who understands the business is better able to exercise responsible self-management, and that work teams able to calculate profits from their own activities improve their own self-governance ability. One such firm sent a work team, rather than a management group, to meet with investment analysts to explain how they were developing new products.

INVESTING IN CAPABILITIES AND TRUST AT THE FIRM LEVEL

Investments in trust at the individual and team levels, of course, accumulate into an investment in trust for the entire firm. Some firms, such as General Electric, have made extensive human capital investments as part of their redesign efforts. Others, such as Johnson & Johnson, have long been recognized for creating a culture in which managers and employees can creatively focus on specific market segments while benefitting themselves and the larger corporation.

At Johnson & Johnson, top management spends several weeks each year carefully evaluating all aspects of the performance of each of the firm's more than one hundred subsidiary companies. A profit-sharing system provides company management with a high level of average compensation, while top management recognizes that rewards must accurately reflect the actual performance of managers, not merely luck or uncontrollable market circumstances. The extensive investments required to maintain the perceived worthiness of the reward system is seen by top management as the key to the firm's overall governance process.

INVESTING IN CAPABILITIES AND TRUST
AT THE NETWORK LEVEL

At the network level, the key trust investments are made across firms (or, in the internal network, across commonly owned but independently managed organizational units). Some of these investments are in actual dollars. For example, Novell, the computer software company, has gained recognition for its willingness to assist suppliers in need of financial help by buying their inventory in advance and settling accounts when deliveries are made.[6]

A similar investment practice is common at Motorola, though it does not involve out-of-pocket dollars.[7] In order to maintain the flow of new equipment it needs to build and test microchips, Motorola has established strategic partnerships with small, highly competent firms specializing in developing such state-of-the-art equipment. These small firms, however, may not have the cash to invest in the design and construction of expensive new manufacturing equipment. Motorola has in several instances extended purchase orders for the future output of these firms. These purchase orders can then be used as collateral by the supplier firms to obtain the funding needed to meet the joint needs of the alliance. Thus, Motorola is investing in trust by taking the risk that suppliers ultimately will be able to deliver on their state-of-the-art designs and never-before-built products.

CONCLUSION

Historically, organizational forms and managerial philosophies have evolved together. Where forms are implemented without supporting philosophies, failures usually occur. In Chapter 10, we examine the difficulties many large, mature firms are currently facing as they seek to realign themselves with their environment and redesign internal structures and processes. The problems these firms face lie not only in the changes that have occurred in their environment but also in the behaviors and attitudes of their managers. Successful redesign will only occur as strategies, structures, processes, and philosophies are brought back into tight fit.

PART FOUR

DYNAMIC FIT:
THE PROCESS OF ORGANIZATIONAL RENEWAL

In the final part of this book, we shift the focus away from understanding and illustration, onto the actions firms should take for their long-term health and success. Previous chapters have described complete recipes for organizational success, carefully detailing competitive strategies, organizational structures, and management processes from the oldest to the newest. The remaining challenge for managers is not only to decide on the appropriate organization form for their company and to make the necessary modifications to the existing system to achieve tight internal and external fit, but also to install the processes that are required to keep the company healthy on a continuing basis.

For a brand-new company, achieving such "dynamic fit" is a tall order. It is even more difficult in existing companies, where the current configuration of strategies, structures, and processes may appear to be more of a maze than a path to success. In Chapter 10, we discuss companies that are struggling to redesign themselves—cutting costs, downsizing, bringing in new management teams, and so on. Unfortunately, many of these companies will not be satisfied with their redesign efforts, primarily because they are not fully aware of the problems they should be solving or the redesign process they should be pursuing. In fact, what may be required is a total redesign.

In Chapter 11, we describe how total redesign may grow more costly in today's fast-paced world. The most successful firms in this competitive environment will learn the skills of self-renewal or continuous redesign. These skills will not only become part of the "learned" know-how of the successful firm, they will also be taught to current as well as future members through the design of the firm and its internal processes.

In the final chapter, we reiterate the prescriptions for fit and their application. More important, we illustrate that fit is no longer an idealistic "ought" but an economic "must"—not only within the firm but throughout the network form and the total global economy.

CHAPTER 10

THE PROCESS OF CORPORATE REDESIGN

Today, many large, mature companies find themselves in the throes of change. In ambitious, sometimes bold efforts to gain control of their future, these companies have implemented one (or more) of the currently popular change programs such as total quality management,[1] process reengineering,[2] and even complete reinvention.[3] Unfortunately, many of these efforts are not very successful. Among the large U.S. firms still struggling to reinvent themselves are IBM, General Motors, and Sears, Roebuck—former Hall of Fame companies. Moreover, even the few companies that have made it through the maelstrom to new goals and achievements—General Electric is perhaps the best example—have done so at a heavy human cost.

Why is the process of redesign in many companies so slow, uncertain, and tortured? Why are even the successes marred by the wounds inflicted on managers and employees—wounds that may take years to heal? We believe that most redesign efforts fail, or achieve only limited success, for three interrelated reasons: (1) the change process is viewed as repair rather than redesign; (2) the managerial philosophies followed in the early phases of the redesign impede future steps; and (3) the new operating logic—the manner in which new strategies, structures, and processes are expected to function—is never fully articulated, nor are its demands on managerial philosophies fully examined.

Our first purpose in this chapter is to discuss how these factors interact to produce a flawed redesign process, from which

159

many prominent firms have not escaped. Our focus, however, is not on how these firms got into their present predicament. Instead, we will describe the redesign process required for them to work themselves out of it.

REPAIR VERSUS REDESIGN

There is a growing conviction, only partially supported by systematic research but fueled by numerous company examples, that major redesigns cannot be undertaken by existing management teams.[4] The basic reason is that top management is committed to its own past decisions and strategies, and it downplays negative feedback in an effort to "stay the course."

We believe that many managers are, in fact, alert to symptoms of organizational breakdown and are quite willing to take the necessary steps to "fix" problems as they appear. They are often unsuccessful, however, because either they assume the basic organizational package is sound and only problem solving is required, or as is more common today, they suspect that the system is inadequate, but it is not clear why or where it is flawed.

The assumption that the organization only needs to be repaired, at least at the beginning of major transition periods, is understandable. It has long been argued that "limited search around known solutions"[5] is not only typical of managerial behavior, but is often a sound way of making the incremental adaptations required by everyday environmental changes.[6] Indeed, small, carefully conceived sequences of incremental adaptation have kept successful firms such as 3M and Procter & Gamble healthy for decades. Moreover, managers may continue to work only on the symptoms of deep, underlying organizational malfunction because these may not produce recognizable evidence of a serious lack of fit in the organization.

However, while today's managers increasingly "feel" that their organizations' strategies and structures may be fundamentally unsound, they may not have the analytical tools to determine what features are inadequate and why, and they also may not have the language to articulate their concerns or diagnosis. That is, in order to see fundamental misalignments between the environment and a firm's strategies and structures, managers must be able to envision alternative organizational forms and to compare the costs and benefits of such forms to those of the organization already in place. Thus, it is not just that managers are wedded to their present organization, but that they have had little reason until the last decade or so to search for new organizational alternatives. Consequently, many managers have had little experience in rethinking the total linkage across their company's environment, strategy, and organization.

Of course, managers discuss efforts at change and new "solutions" with other managers, but they are often attracted only to pieces of the process that capture their imagination, rather than to a broad, alternative organizational approach. Moreover, because so few firms today are successfully exploring truly new alternatives, there is a scarcity of fundamental redesign options for managers to consider. Books and programs touting quality improvement, customer service, supplier partnerships, and staff downsizing abound, but these are not, even in their broadest applications, options for total redesign.

In general, we believe that managers focus on treating the symptoms of organizational maladies because they already have remedies in stock, and because the real ailment may not be visible. Moreover, even if they suspect a serious underlying illness, they may not understand its pathology, its prognosis, or its cure. In fact, many managers have rarely seen a truly healthy organization and thus find it difficult to recognize how and why their own structures and processes are malfunctioning.

Beginning in the early 1980s, for example, Eastman Kodak responded to a series of earnings declines with a program of acquisitions designed to generate technical and financial synergy, while at the same time cutting back its work force and creating a lean, divisionalized organization. However, the effort to derive synergies among diverse ventures in biotechnology, digital imaging, data storage, batteries, and so forth resulted in an increase in corporate planning staff. Therefore, corporate overhead grew as other personnel were being cut. At least five subsequent "restructurings" intended to fix Kodak's problems have produced little bottom-line improvement, while allegedly damaging employee morale and motivation. Decisions made within the last two years appear to be pushing Kodak to refocus on its core business, photographic and related products, while seeking greater efficiency in overall resource utilization. Whether these moves are merely further efforts at "fixing" the old organization or represent an integrated new system is not yet clear. In any event, Kodak, as well as many other prominent American firms, may need to change its mind-set from repair to redesign.

REGRESSIVE MANAGERIAL PHILOSOPHIES

Even in firms whose managers have recognized the need for redesign and are experimenting with broad new approaches, change programs may go awry because managers' own philosophies are posing an unrecognized barrier to successful implementation. Indeed, the severity of current competitive challenges seems to have produced a regression in managerial ideology—a retreat to earlier beliefs and behaviors. This regression has been visible in the statements and actions of several prominent chief executives over the past decade. Indeed, in firm after firm, a common scenario has been played out.

For many top managers in firms suffering a severe decline in competitive position, the harsh criticism this brings from various external constituents is a first-time experience. Often the initial careful, and perhaps halting, actions of these managers further increases the hostility of the firm's stakeholders. Finally, in the full grip of both economic and emotional crisis, such managers' first major move is deep cost cutting—typically resulting in across-the-board reductions in middle managers and employees.

Managers' behaviors and pronouncements in the early response stage are often remarkably similar to those of turn-of-the-century managers following the traditional management philosophy. That is, in their statements, managers accept no responsibility for the problems at hand, nor do they defend the contributions of those who are being let go. Virtually all key operating decisions are pulled upward to the corporate level and often are made without wide consultation. Managers may acknowledge some mistakes but rationalize them as a necessary price to pay given the firm's financial distress. Further, they may say or imply that only those at the top of the company have the perspective (and perhaps the knowledge and skill) needed to make key decisions.

The early period of across-the-board reductions in staff is usually followed by growing managerial recognition of, and concern for, the impact these cuts have on employee morale and motivation. Although tough talk may still be used to assuage investors, the tone inside begins to sound much like that of the human relationists of the 1930s and the 1940s. Management urges the firm's remaining members to "pull together to get us through this trying period," and it praises members for the loyalty and effort they have demonstrated over the years, proclaiming its intention to remember and reward those contributions when the current crisis is over.

Many executives in large struggling companies appear to employ such regressive managerial philosophies and practices unwittingly. Vacillation between the rhetoric and behaviors of the traditional and human relations periods is common among managers in today's troubled firms. First, a rash of apparently dispassionate, unilateral cuts occurs, followed by appeals for involvement and cooperation. Then more cuts are made, followed by more appeals. And so on. Of course, such vacillation produces the same responses today that it did in earlier times. Organization members may appreciate the opportunity to discuss pressing issues with top management, but most have doubts about the depth of management's support and the sincerity of its promises. Indeed, in the face of members' fears about job security, management efforts to rebuild lines of communication and restore commitment are generally viewed as at best patronizing and at worst manipulative.

In sum, managers' regression to the philosophies and behaviors of earlier periods, and their movement back and forth between unilateral actions and efforts at damage control, have two predictable outcomes. First, the concerns and suspicions aroused by their behavior hamper current operations. Second, and even more important, the cynicism engendered by this behavior erodes the base of trust necessary to create and implement the new strategies, structures, and processes required for future corporate success.

SUCCESSFUL REDESIGN: TOTAL AND CONTINUOUS

The barriers to redesign created by treating the process as mere problem solving, or by reverting to unilateral and patronizing attitudes and behaviors when an attempt is made at major change, are undoubtedly hampering companies' efforts to respond to today's challenging competitive environment. However, even those firms that have recognized the need for revolutionary change, and have survived the human costs of dramatic downsizing may still not be on the road to successful redesign. Indeed, as noted earlier, only a fraction of the major U.S. firms in trouble have achieved an adaptive capacity capable of providing both current operating stability and the ability to respond to the continuing challenges of the 1990s and beyond. For the vast majority of struggling firms, a final barrier remains: the task of visualizing, understanding, and communicating the strategy, organizational structure, and management philosophy and processes required by a total redesign.

XEROX CORPORATION:
A COMPLETE RECOVERY?[7]

In Chapter 3, we discussed three companies that engaged in major redesign efforts: Chrysler Corporation, Harley-Davidson, and General Electric. Each company weathered its worst years and now appears to be on a firm footing. Another well-known firm, however, is in the midst of recovery and therefore is a useful case study of adaptation. This firm is the Xerox Corporation.

The path to recovery at Xerox has not been smooth, but it has been steady. Despite the technical brilliance of its research and development group, Xerox was crippled in the 1970s by the low-cost copiers introduced by Japanese manufacturers. Xerox's loss of market share was followed by ill-advised ventures into unrelated businesses such as financial services. Its redesign process began not with a bold stroke but with what former Xerox CEO David Kearns characterized as a "long-march" emphasis on quality. The push toward total quality management at Xerox has created positive results because it has been embedded in an organization that emphasizes not only team empowerment but also rewards tied directly to measures of customer satisfaction. The focus on quality and customer service was given further impetus in the early 1990s with the creation of "microenterprise units" led by teams that have complete responsibility for work processes designed around key products (the failure to get promising new products to market has been a continuing problem at Xerox). In fact, the company was broken into nine product divisions—actually a matrix of nearly independent businesses, three each in copiers, printers, and software/services. Current CEO Paul Allaire claims that the new organization gives "everyone in the company a direct line of sight to the customer."

Although progress was made in process and product design, the company's overall resources were diluted by poorly performing acquisitions in financial services. Xerox's full refocusing on its core businesses—giving renewed meaning to its claim to be "the document company"—occurred only recently with the divestiture of the profit-draining financial services businesses. With that burden removed, Xerox has now moved heavily into high-speed digital copiers and printers, and has begun joint ventures with Microsoft to market new lines of printers, copiers, and fax machines and with Sun Microsystems to build printers for its computer workstations. The latest venture puts the Xerox name on a wide range of products for the home office, products provided by subcontractors and sold through supermarkets.

In all, Xerox is attempting to fulfill its long-time promise to be the leading provider of innovative "document" products by designing an organization that has a strong linkage from the laboratory to the customer. To date, Xerox has clearly made progress, but it remains behind Canon in copier market share and has not yet fully shed its image as the company that originated but failed to develop the laser printer, personal computer, and fax machine.

At GE, Chrysler, and Harley-Davidson, and increasingly at Xerox, not only have turnarounds been achieved in profitability, but a new confidence has also been forged in the viability of the logic guiding the new fit among these firms' strategy, structure, and management processes. Nevertheless, despite their current levels of accomplishment, it is not yet clear that any of these firms has completed the redesign process. To be complete, these firms—and other large, mature companies in similar circumstances—must proceed through three key milestones in the redesign process.

KEY MILESTONES
IN CORPORATE REDESIGN

The first milestone, which for most firms will follow a significant staff reduction, is to rearticulate the company's distinctive competence—to decide where the company belongs on the industry value chain and who its primary customers are. For Chrysler, this meant a return to a more limited product line to which the company can apply its engineering expertise. At Xerox, the center of gravity is the research and development team. Units and processes that are not central to the full utilization of the firm's distinctive competence must be either eliminated or considered as candidates for outsourcing.

The second milestone is to *establish the logic and organization* by which the company can use its core competencies to deliver products and services to the marketplace. For some companies, this is a process of rediscovery. General Electric, for example, found renewed life in its own earlier organizational form. It essentially stripped away the corporate impediments (e.g., financial and planning specialists) to its formerly viable divisional organization, which it allowed to operate as it used to— and as this form should.

Finally, in every successful redesign, firms need to *specify and practice a managerial philosophy* that ties together the remodeled organization. As the redesign process progressed at Chrysler, Harley-Davidson, General Electric, and Xerox, top managers at each firm began to rearticulate a human resources managerial philosophy—restating their confidence in the value and capabilities of managers and employees and reinforcing their beliefs that employees could and would exercise self-direction and self-control in the pursuit of company goals. Each of the companies expanded its training programs to upgrade member technical and self-governance skills, and sought to broaden responsibilities at all levels. At Chrysler, quality programs sought to tap skills at all employee levels; at Harley-Davidson, work teams were taught to calculate and employ statistical process quality control; at General Electric, investments were made in team building and education in "business" skills, as well as in technical competence. Moreover, top managers attributed current success to the full utilization of member competencies, and they projected future achievements based on even broader skill development and utilization. While not every management statement was sincere, and some efforts to tap employee ideas and initiatives were made primarily to enhance morale and increase cooperation (in line with the human relations philosophy), enough substance accompanied the management rhetoric to support the redesign process. Indeed, at Xerox, it may well be that its long-standing commitment to a human resources philosophy of management has been the one sustaining feature amongst a series of market and investment mistakes.

THE ACID TEST OF REDESIGN

The first real test of a total redesign process and its supporting managerial philosophy will not occur until the firm demonstrates its ability to sustain its newly created organization and its newly found success under a new management team. If the operating logic of the firm and its supporting managerial philosophy are owned only by top management, they will depart with that team. On the other hand, if the new logic and philosophy have been articulated and widely accepted—if they have been "built into" decision-making mechanisms and criteria—the new design may survive the loss of charismatic leaders and the transition to a new management team.

CONCLUSION

Total, continuous redesign is a difficult task for any firm, and it is particularly challenging to those companies that have achieved great size and success in their current organizational form. Nevertheless, future success, if not actual survival, may well depend on how quickly and clearly these companies recognize that their present systems cannot be repaired but must be replaced by a new design that fits the demands of today's environment.

Firms that do succeed will not only develop new strategies and structures that meet competitive demands, they will also build a new managerial philosophy, one that will guide them toward the ability to adapt continually. By investing in the long-term growth and development of all their human assets, these firms will create organizations that are capable of self-renewal. It is this topic to which we turn in Chapter 11.

CHAPTER 11

THE SELF-RENEWING ORGANIZATION:

Learning and Teaching Adaptation

In Chapter 10 we highlighted the challenges embedded in the process of major organizational redesign—challenges of such magnitude that managers can only face them with the thought that, once the redesign is complete, the organization will be set for the foreseeable future. Indeed, in previous decades, firms that survived the redesign process necessitated by major technical or market "revolutions" often were able to operate for extended periods by making only small, "evolutionary" changes in strategy and structure.

There is growing awareness, however, that the period between revolutions is getting shorter, perhaps even disappearing into what has been called "permanent white water."[1] Today's periods of fine-tuning have, for most organizations, taken on the appearance of yesterday's periods of major change.

In a world of constant challenge and change, the search focuses on ways to give organizations the capability to continuously test and adjust their external and internal fit. In such a world, total redesigns such as those described in Chapter 10 will only occur in those firms that have failed to learn adaptive skills. In today's fast-paced competitive environment, firms cannot allow their strategies to slip further and further out of alignment with the market, causing pressure for a "dramatic new approach." Managers cannot allow structural and process impediments to grow ever larger, stifling productivity and blocking their view of the market and its needs.

Instead, it is commonly recognized today, that organizations need to learn how to be self-renewing—to constantly develop and upgrade their competencies to meet the environment's demands, both large and small. Firms that have built the capability to continually redesign their strategies and structures have become what some call "learning organizations." These organizations not only can and do change; they also appear to have a superior understanding of the process of change.[2]

In this chapter, we will give operational meaning to the concept of organizational self-renewal. In the process, we will suggest that in addition to exploring the concept of the learning organization, it may be equally if not more useful to examine the notion of the "teaching organization." This distinction is not just a play on words. Organizations themselves do not learn, the people in them do. However, organizations do teach—their policies and mechanisms encourage specific behaviors, and their incentives and control systems reinforce choices. Thus, if we want organizations to be self-renewing, we must make certain that they are programmed to teach and reward adaptive behaviors on the part of their members.

THE SUBSTANCE OF RENEWAL

Before we begin to explore renewal through both teaching and learning, we need to specify what organizational assets may need to be renewed. True organizational renewal does not focus on financial or technical resources, although responding to radical shifts in the environment may call for new and flexible sources of credit, and technological breakthroughs may accelerate the need for new equipment and manufacturing processes. Instead, the prime target of renewal is the organization's core or distinctive competence—its package of skills, know-how, and other intangible resources whose application adds value to a business in a manner not easily matched by competitors.

DYNAMIC CAPABILITY

Tangible assets alone do not usually provide a sustainable competitive advantage. For example, a patent provides a temporary, unique resource, but it is the skill and knowledge that produced the patented product (and that will presumably generate others) that gives the organization what economist David Teece and his associates have called a "dynamic capability."[3] Similarly, access to financial resources may give a firm an initial advantage, but the ability to apply that resource creatively in order to generate the returns that will ensure its renewal is the key to long-term success.

Indeed, assets are the most transparent part of the package that makes up an organization's distinctive competence. Equipment, capital, sources of supply and distribution, even the technical skills and knowledge possessed by the firm's engineers and scientists, are visible to competitors and invite imitation. Far less easily matched, however, is the company's know-how, its deep understanding of the operating logic embedded in the organizational form the company has chosen to use. Such an intangible asset is considerably less visible to the competitor's prying eye, and is valuable only because it is an integral part of the total organizational and managerial package.

ARTICULATING DISTINCTIVE COMPETENCE

For a firm to renew, develop, and expand its distinctive competence, it must know what that is. Surprisingly, not every firm knows this, or at least not every firm can articulate what has made it successful. In fact, a common feature among successful companies is the degree to which they self-consciously describe, discuss, and seek to inculcate in their members the most important keys to their effectiveness. Of course, simply stating and attempting to teach "our way" does not guarantee success; many unsuccessful organizations are adamant about knowing and following rules and procedures. What is important is that the message has embedded in it not only the what, but also the why and how of success. Frequently, the message is "stored" in a myth—an often-told, exaggerated story or example that captures the essence of a firm's success.

For example, at 3M Company, the press for product innovation has created a collection of well-known stories, some with probably only a hint of factual content, describing the successful ideas that almost got away because someone failed to pursue them or would not consider them. At Hewlett-Packard, the story of the recruit from another firm who, after suggesting to a group of HP engineers that they prepare a research proposal on an idea under discussion, receives the response, "We don't need to ask, we'll just do it," was long a valued part of company folklore. For first-to-market Prospector firms like 3M and Hewlett-Packard, myths about distinctive competence usually turn on displays of almost rebellious creativity. In efficiency-oriented Defender firms, myths glorify the junior clerk who suggests a million-dollar savings procedure or the engineer who patiently explains how a new machine is not needed and an old one can be adapted to outperform the newest model. For myths to last, however, they must reflect underlying truths—they must caricature real features of the firm's distinctive competence.

In some instances, a firm's distinctive know-how may not be easily captured in a single myth. At Procter & Gamble, key features of the firm's organizational and management approaches have long been recognized as crucial to success, even as "proprietary" knowledge. The ability of Procter & Gamble to move quickly and effectively into overseas markets is usually explained as resulting from its willingness to "recreate" the parent firm in every country—that is, to allow country-by-country adaptations in product design, packaging, and advertising—to reflect local conditions. At the other end of the value chain, Procter & Gamble has long treated its skill in the development of self-managing work teams in the company's manufacturing plants as proprietary know-how. Similarly, at Johnson & Johnson, many managers attribute the company's long success to its ability to grant subsidiary companies extensive operating autonomy through joint goal setting between corporate and subsidiary managers, as well as to an end-of-year performance review that ties rewards to controllable performance. And at Texas Instruments, as noted earlier, detailed understanding of the steps required to move a product from a developmental project to long-term manufacturing efficiency is treasured as a proprietary competence.

When the distinctive competence of a firm is an intangible asset such as a major structural innovation, an innovative managerial philosophy, or a creative and farsighted understanding of the technical forces shaping an industry, it is frequently useful to articulate it in written form. Thus, at Texas Instruments, the transition process was recorded in both lengthy policy statements and pamphlet form. At Lincoln Electric, James F. Lincoln's writings, including his book *Incentive Management*,[4] provided a clear statement of a farsighted managerial philosophy that has guided the firm since its founding, emphasizing the belief that employees are capable of responsible and self-directed behavior and that they will produce high-quality, high-volume output if given the opportunity and rewarded significantly. At Intel, all three members of the founding team produced books reflecting their experiences and philosophies, and at Johnson & Johnson, the company creed remains an important operating document.

THE PROCESS OF RENEWAL

Firms that understand and articulate the sources of their distinctive competence are often more than halfway to the goal of sustained excellence. Nevertheless, the process is not complete unless the knowledge is used. Renewal can be initiated internally—for example, by an executive action or mechanism that lays the firm's understanding of its competencies up against its current performance. However, purely internal reevaluation runs the risk of finding only what top management wants to hear. Thus, successful firms frequently engage in external reviews—bringing in outsiders to evaluate whether the firm is maintaining and applying its competencies. Finally, some firms appear to have built the renewal process directly into their operations—they have found ways of continuing to apply their distinctive competencies in a broader and broader arena.

By themselves, internal reviews have frequently not been sufficient to sustain organizational excellence. It is simply too easy, for example, to let review mechanisms such as periodic surveys, quarterly retreats, and annual reports become routine, and even to be transformed into public relations mechanisms rather than instruments of tough-minded assessment. An exception occurred at Johnson & Johnson in the 1980s when its CEO demanded that managers throughout the firm review the company creed and determine whether or not it was still a useful guide. That process sparked serious debate, which fortunately was fresh in the minds of all Johnson & Johnson managers when the Tylenol tampering incidents occurred. The immediate, unquestioned response of removing the product from store shelves provided proof, both internally and externally, that the creed was still an operational document—because the CEO had enabled it to be such.

External reviews are common in the public sector but are seldom undertaken in private firms, except as required by law or regulation. The inspector general, the General Accounting Office, and the grand jury may not only focus on adherence to rules and regulations but also offer broad commentary on the application of competencies. A few public agencies and private companies have begun to seek help from consultants, either to conduct a broad appraisal of the organization's performance or to assist internal officers in determining whether they are continuing to utilize their organizations' capabilities effectively. Increasingly, successful firms are drawing customers and suppliers into the appraisal process. One could argue that sales data provide enough information on customer satisfaction, but loyal customers often abandon a firm only after their repeated efforts to be heard have failed. Similarly, one might expect that suppliers have little incentive to offer constructive criticism, but many firms are now finding that upstream expertise is readily forthcoming and highly valuable.

Building the renewal process directly into the operation of the firm has some ultimate limit. For years, Hewlett-Packard renewed itself by splitting new divisions off from older operations when they had successfully created new products or markets. HP's continuous technology-driven divisional growth not only brought the company financial success; it also demonstrated that the process of bringing good science to the business marketplace worked and that every engineer could develop his or her own product and run his or her own division.

Similarly, at Johnson & Johnson, over a hundred and fifty subsidiary companies represent both acquisitions and spin-offs, and provide small-firm opportunities for rapid managerial development and big-firm opportunities for investing it. However, even in firms such as Hewlett-Packard and Johnson & Johnson, there are limits to the pace of expansion and the ability of corporate headquarters to recognize and evaluate new opportunities.

On the other hand, a firm such as Corning has produced an almost unlimited arena for the application of its technical and managerial competencies. By continuing to create alliances, the firm has taken itself into myriad industries, complementing the skills and knowledge of other firms and in the process expanding its own repertoire. Indeed, continually expanding and changing interactions is the major advantage the network form brings to the renewal process. (We will explore the special features of network firm renewal at the end of this chapter.)

LEARNING TO RENEW

An organization's know-how is stored not only in the minds of its members but also in various organizational processes and characteristics. Indeed, organizations regularly attempt to codify successful behaviors into standard operating procedures and to delineate the logic supporting those procedures in statements of company policy. Procedures and policies, along with the supporting myths described earlier, are part of the overall culture of the organization —the collective "way we operate."

An organization's way of operating is passed along to new-comers by their superiors and peers as well as by the documents that describe the company's processes and approaches. In fact, as we have maintained throughout this book, the total package of structural features and operating systems by which organization members carry out their work is itself a preset problem-solving approach.

Today, when managers and management scholars talk about "organizational learning," they are usually describing the processes by which organization members become conscious not only of what to do and how to do it, but *why* it is being done. That is, when members move outside the operating lessons embedded in the organization's current structure and systems and begin the search for new ways to think about what they are doing, they move into what Chris Argyris and Donald Schon, describing their concept of "double loop" learning, call the outer loop.[5] When organization members have the capability, through internal change mechanisms and/or external reviews, to under-stand the logic of their current approaches and test them against meaningful alternatives, the organization then has the capacity to "learn"—to reshape structures, systems, and procedures either to allow existing competencies to flourish or to accommo-date new competencies.

If members can knowledgeably adapt their behaviors, and if those behaviors are then made part of the organization's mes-sage to newcomers, the organization can be said to have learned. If the organization's members become adept at the change process and the organization's mechanisms facilitate that skill, the "learning organization" is on its way to becoming a reality. In such an organization, according to noted management writer and consultant Tom Peters, members learn to embrace change.[6]

TEACHING THE RENEWAL PROCESS

While organization members are learning to learn, the organiza-tion, as it presently exists, continues to teach. That is, until they are changed, the organization's existing structures and systems continue to shape the attitudes and behaviors of its members.

As an organization member, I learn from my interaction with the system. Each time the organization responds to my behavior, it shapes my future actions. If I work hard to prepare a report and then discover that it was ignored in the subsequent decision-making process, I may work with less thoroughness and commitment on the next report. On the other hand, if my creativity is rewarded with recognition and resources, I will strive to be creative in the future. If I am given information, training, and opportunity, I will do my best to reciprocate with outstanding performance. If I am given orders without explanation and am provided with little or no feedback on the outcome of my performance, I will work with ever-declining effort. In short, I learn from what I am taught by the organization.

If management recognizes that the organization is a "teaching machine," its task becomes making certain that the machine is programmed to reinforce desired outcomes and behaviors. A savvy management will be careful in designing the organization's teaching program—the way it is set up to respond to, reward, and shape members' behavior.

Clearly, the notion of programming, or reprogramming, the organization to provide appropriate feedback is easier to prescribe than to practice. Indeed, even in well-managed firms, the organization does not give consistent reinforcement over time throughout all areas. Left alone, the system will diverge from one unit to the next, sometimes rewarding continued adherence to procedures that no longer generate the desired results. In fact, in most organizations, management attention to the lessons the organization is teaching is shallow and sporadic. Obviously, management cannot spend its time determining the message associated with every behavior. However, there are three key parts of the teaching "program" to which successful, self-renewing firms appear to give major attention: (1) directly building renewal into all performance and decision-making criteria; (2) explicitly keying rewards not only to current performance but also to the continuous development of new capability; and

(3) visibly investing in the creation of expanded competency, including not only improved equipment and technical training but also expanded business and managerial know-how at all organizational levels.

BUILDING RENEWAL INTO PERFORMANCE CRITERIA

Successful firms not only develop clear decision-making and performance criteria, they usually build into these a developmental component. For example, 3M Company has for some time built a measure of product innovation into its performance review procedure. A minimum of 25 percent of the annual sales of every division is expected to be generated from products introduced within the past five years. At 3M, that policy leaves no question about whether new ideas are to be stimulated and supported— they must be to meet division performance standards.

At Rubbermaid, an almost identical criterion was installed by former CEO Stanley Gault. His demanding performance goal of having 30 percent of sales generated from products less than five years old was consistently met during the 1980s. During that decade, Rubbermaid was generating approximately three hundred new products a year, including entirely new lines. Each of Rubbermaid's operating divisions is a major contributor to this achievement, and, based on their special competencies, divisions are expected to enter a new market segment every eighteen to twenty-four months.[7]

For decades, Lincoln Electric has expected its product line to be offered each year with improved performance capability at or below the previous year's price. Lincoln has simply sought to pass along to its customers a portion of the benefits of a continuous improvement learning curve. To achieve this goal, the company has explicitly sought annual improvements in every performance category. This unending company goal has been supported by improvements in equipment and methods made by both managers and employees.

At General Electric, the criterion for measuring dynamic capability is much broader but equally explicit. The requirement that each GE business hold the position of either the number one or number two performer in that industry is, in effect, a measure of continuous renewal of core competencies. If an operating unit loses the capability to add value at a level that will keep it at the top of its peer group, a management change and/or divestment is sure to follow. The operating units are thus highly motivated to focus not only on immediate output data but also on the steps needed to sustain a leading level of performance.

The common feature of these firms is the explicitness—the uncompromising clarity—of their performance criteria. A related and equally important feature is continuity. The criteria have remained in place long enough to guarantee that they are considered important and that they will be applied consistently and continuously. Neither of these features is common in the typical organization. While statements emphasizing the importance of creativity and progress are common, explicit requirements for the development of new products and services on a continuing basis are uncommon enough to be newsworthy. Such criteria, of course, cannot be frivolously invoked. They must both represent crucial aspects of the firm's market strategy and reflect foundation skills and competencies that management can draw out and build upon. Moreover, many organizations that launch renewal efforts do not sustain them. Indeed, many such efforts emerge under the label of "programs," suggesting that the emphasis on developing new products or services will be temporary.

Explicit performance criteria focused on development and renewal are difficult to construct and legitimize. They are easy to let slide as long as current earnings are adequate. Perhaps this is why so few firms have them in place, and why those that do are often among the most admired organizations.

KEYING REWARDS TO CONTINUOUS COMPETENCY DEVELOPMENT

Not surprisingly, the development and renewal criteria at companies such as 3M and Rubbermaid are taken seriously because they form the basis on which the company appraises management and unit performance. Managers and units that excel in continuing innovation receive clearly specified rewards of significant size.

Sometimes the reward system is companywide. American West, an airline built on the notion that it could successfully compete against the industry giants only by developing and using fully the abilities of all its members, shares 15 percent of pretax profits, paid quarterly, with its employees. Sharing is across-the-board because nearly all employees are cross-trained in a variety of skills and operations, and they regularly do what needs to be done in a self-managing manner. Moreover, employees now have a 30 percent ownership stake in the company, created by stock purchases and the sort of stock-option plans usually reserved for senior executives. Similarly, in the Brazilian firm Semco, all units participate in a profit-sharing plan that distributes approximately one quarter of after-tax profits. More important, each member knows how and why the profit was earned. Every month, employees are given a balance sheet, a profit and loss statement, and a cash-flow statement for their respective units, which they have been taught to read in classes run by their own union.[8]

In an even more direct approach, 3M employees are not only rewarded handsomely for product innovations, they are also often given the opportunity to follow their ideas well beyond the development process. At AT&T, managers from supervisors to department heads are given the opportunity to back their ideas and suggestions with some portion of their own salary. Returns, keyed to the portion of salary invested, can reach a maximum of eight times a manager's annual salary for successful ventures.

Not surprisingly, given its decades of growth and financial success, Johnson & Johnson attempts through its joint goal-setting process to incorporate specific developmental goals into the annual operating objectives of each of its subsidiary companies. These objectives form the basis for the potentially enormous annual bonuses units can earn from superior performance, providing they have also met specific long-term development criteria. Similarly, just as they have since the turn of the century, employees of Lincoln Electric continue to earn performance-based bonuses that bring their average income to twice the national average for their job categories. Of course, they should earn twice as much, given that they are responsible for quality control, production control, materials and tool control, and so on. It is their ongoing commitment and creativity that continues to renew the company and its products.

Increasingly, firms are rediscovering the value of performance-based rewards at all levels. The more thoughtful firms are aware that designing effective performance-based reward systems is a continuing process, one that forces the firm to align individual and team work assignments with corporate needs and expectations, and to tie pay plans carefully to factors over which members have some control. Good reward plans are never finished; they must be discussed and honed each year to make sure they are still rewarding effective performance and are still viewed as legitimate by all members.

Beyond the basics of good reward system design, self-renewing firms such as those described here make continuing development a key part of the reward system. They work with individuals and groups to set objectives that demand reevaluation and renewal efforts, and they measure and reward the accomplishment of those objectives. To this point, few firms have gone far enough. For example, while no firm would think of letting a year go by without a careful appraisal of profit performance and assessment of assets, most firms give little thought to "auditing" of internal consistency in their core processes or analyzing how extensively their intended market strategy is understood throughout the company. Structural fit and a common understanding of strategy are known to be shared properties of highly successful firms, found as consistently as the most prized financial ratios. Nevertheless, firms that regularly pay attention to the hard numbers often ignore the other aspects of distinctive competence. One firm that does focus on both its tangible and intangible assets is Nike. A recent survey showed Nike employees to have the highest levels of understanding and acceptance of company mission and policies ever recorded by the national firm that conducted the study.[9]

INVESTING IN A DYNAMIC CAPABILITY

Successful firms tend to specify development and innovation criteria, and to key rewards to the achievement of explicit objectives. Also, they are willing to make large, visible investments in the time, training, and other resources needed to sustain their core competencies.

Investments of time for creativity and renewal are often ignored, even in firms that say they support them. However, in those firms where the evidence of companywide creativity and renewal is highly visible, there is frequently explicit recognition that such an investment of time is needed. At 3M Company, everyone is free to use—in fact, is expected to use—up to 15 percent of company time working on ideas for new products. Moreover, recognizing that even with its commitment to creativity there is still a chance that ideas will be overlooked, 3M holds periodic "fairs" where representatives of various units come together to hear about ideas that may not have been pursued throughout the company. Frequently, an idea will be "sold" at such meetings, perhaps after being embellished in conversation and analyzed by a unit with different technologies and markets. Investments in both time and training are made at Chaparral Steel, where the intent is to spend as much as a third of every organization member's time in technical, business, and self-governance education.

U.S. firms in general tend to lag well behind their German and Japanese counterparts in investments in training, particularly at the lower levels of the organization. Of course, it is just such training that provides the broad know-how for sustained performance. Again, it is not surprising that the successful firms described throughout this book are among the leaders in training and education investments. Southwest Air creates its fully cross-trained customer service representatives by investing in a minimum of eighteen weeks of training, but the returns are obvious as personnel move easily from in-flight service to check in, baggage handling, reservations, and so on.

We believe that continuous training will be increasingly recognized as the most direct investment that firms can make in building a dynamic capability. Many companies have long recognized the value of such investment at the professional and managerial levels. Of course, the shelf life of technical and scientific knowledge grows shorter with each passing decade. Therefore, investment quantities and approaches that might have been sufficient in 1990 may be inadequate by the turn of the century.

While most companies recognize the need for training and development of managers and staff professionals, heavy, innovative investments at the work-team level are still rare enough to attract wide attention.[10] Indeed, it may well be that most companies are not yet prepared to view lower-level individuals and teams as key assets. However, failure to invest at this level will most certainly impede flexibility and creativity, two key elements that increasingly underlie company success.

Beyond investments in time and training, firms must invest in the resources needed to sustain their capabilities. Rubbermaid's investment in separate R&D groups at each of its divisions is just such a conscious decision. So too was the long-followed practice at Hewlett-Packard that returned a portion of each division's profits directly to the division, to be used for more R&D without corporate intervention. Indeed, as noted earlier, companies such as Motorola are prepared to invest in outside resources, raising the overall level of resources available to them from the network.

RENEWAL IN NETWORK ORGANIZATIONS

Firms that operate in network organizations may lean naturally toward self-renewal. In networks, the fact that many activities occur across boundaries and are the product of voluntary agreements guided by market forces rather than central plans produces a bias toward effective renewal. Indeed, a firm's core competence is constantly being subjected to market-test questions: Can it provide the continuously more creative and cost-effective goods and services that its network partners expect? Do its internal arrangements facilitate quick and efficient connections with partners? Are the prices and product quality of its internal units able to meet those of outside competitors? These types of questions are before the network firm almost daily.

In a centrally planned firm, an internal disorder may be recognized but given low priority. In a network, every internal disorder comes quickly to the surface and demands immediate attention. Ideally, upstream and downstream partners are quick to point out a given firm's neglect of developmental needs. Technological information and managerial know-how are passed freely through the system—every partner wants every other current and potential partner to be healthy today and tomorrow.

Moreover, the fact that relationships in networks are voluntary—that elements that interact along the value chain have alternatives—helps keep the concepts of distinctive competence and dynamic capability in the mind of every network member. Firms in networks remain valued, fully utilized partners only to the extent that they apply their know-how in a consistently creative manner. Networks lower barriers to entry. Yesterday's skills and assets do not guarantee tomorrow's success. Development—continuous self-renewal—becomes a normal way of life for all members.

In sum, in successful network firms, the "teaching program" for self-renewal is built into the structure itself. Because key interactions are external and visible, firms are positioned on both the inner and outer learning loops. And because interactions are voluntary and self-controlled, firms are forced to take responsibility for their own actions.

Conclusion

Much of the writing on organizational learning and renewal has a seductively patriotic ring to it. Yes, it would be desirable for organizations to be continually adaptable, so their members would not have to go through the large and emotionally wrenching upheavals that were widespread in the 1980s. Fortunately, the path to programmed adaptation is clearly marked and available to any organization that wishes to take it. Companies such as 3M and Johnson & Johnson, which understand the managerial requirements of the adaptive process, can serve as role models. Further, companies such as Corning, that choose to organize as a network will find that continuous adaptation is a natural by-product of that structure. In the final chapter, we offer to companies that wish to use state-of-the-art organizational forms a series of guidelines about how to proceed.

CHAPTER 12

FROM IDEALISTIC OUGHTS TO ECONOMIC MUSTS

This book has centered on the concept and process of discovering and maintaining fit—strategic fit between the organization and its environment and internal fit among strategy, structure, and management processes. Fit, we have argued, is not merely important; it is crucial. With fit comes fame, with misfit comes failure. Fit is not an after-the-fact rationalization for whatever pieces of strategy, structure, and process a firm may have chosen to combine. It is a clear, thoughtfully pursued logic. While it may evolve, it does so with clear purpose and widespread awareness.

We have shown that fit is a simple concept but not a simple process. To achieve strategic fit, organizations must create, understand, develop, and sustain a distinctive competence that adds high value to goods or services the market desires. To achieve internal fit, companies must have a deep understanding of the operating logic linking strategies with structures and processes. Finally, managers' own philosophies of management must fit—they must facilitate rather than impede the leadership style and the decision-making approach required by the chosen strategy and structure.

In this final chapter, we have three objectives. First, we briefly revisit and reemphasize some key issues in the achievement of tight fit. Second, we reiterate the four basic recipes for applying the concept of fit. Finally, we pull together and make clear those areas where we believe managers have choices and those where they don't as we approach the twenty-first century.

CREATING AND MAINTAINING TIGHT FIT

In the continuing pursuit of tight fit, there are three basic guidelines managers can profitably follow. First, be parsimonious—choose the simplest strategy-structure-process form that will bring the company's competencies to bear on market opportunities. Second, understand fully the limits of the chosen strategy and structure—know what they can and cannot do. Third, specify the growth strategy compatible with the chosen organizational form and the criteria for determining when growth threatens the form's current operating limits.

THE ELEGANCE OF FIT

In the world of design, lasting elegance is often associated with simplicity. Organizations with tight fit have their own elegance. Tight-fit firms know what they are good at doing, and they arrange themselves to get it done easily and gracefully. There are few nonfunctional appendages in such firms, and little wasted effort.

As we have illustrated, there are only a limited number of competitive strategies—a limited number of ways to approach a given market. Tight-fit firms choose their strategy—a set of skills and know-how that can be honed to give them a competitive advantage—to fit their distinctive competence. Firms that mix strategies often execute none of them well, because their competencies are spread too thin. Similarly, there are only a limited number of ways to organize, a limited set of structures and processes from which to choose. Each strategy can be served only by those structures whose arrangement of resources and operating logic fit its demands. The combinations that work are few in number. Nevertheless, firms regularly adopt structural features and internal processes that may be sound in and of themselves but fit neither the operating logic of their basic structural form nor their strategy.

In its final shape, every organization is different from every other. One firm will have some idiosyncratic competencies that can only be brought to bear on the market through a clever organizational twist. Another will create a brilliant coordination mechanism that is uniquely suited to its particular customer set and internal systems. A third will modify a structural feature to accommodate a favored but unusual upstream relationship, and so on. Nevertheless, at the core of every tight-fit firm is a consistent, recognizable strategy-structure-process combination. Its operating logic is simple, visible, and understandable.

UNDERSTANDING THE LIMITS

Awkward combinations of strategy, structure, and process emerge not only because managers make poor initial choices, but also because managers do not understand or accept the natural limitations of particular strategies or structures. As we have noted, strategies have clear limits—successful diversification, for example, usually falls well within the financial, technical, and operating know-how of a given firm. Each organizational structure also has its particular limitations. Centrally coordinated functional structures tolerate little variation in product or service design. Divisional structures tolerate only limited amounts of interunit coordination. Nevertheless, despite the fact that these limits are well documented, each generation of managers appears bent on testing for themselves the limits of their organizations.

Limits are often exceeded, we believe, because managers normally do not stop to test whether they have reached or are approaching the limits of the operating logic of a given organizational form. Even when managers sense that they are nearing an operating edge, they may choose to shore up a modification "temporarily," without considering the long-term consequences or costs. Most troubling is the widely held belief that any organizational form can be perfected—that it need not have weaknesses. Thus, managers attempt to remove the cost of redundancy inherent in the divisional organization by centrally planning the sharing of key resources among divisions. Such efforts override the operating logic of the divisional form and cause it either to fail or to succeed only at unreasonably high cost. Similarly, managers in an efficiency-oriented functional organization may attempt to force the structure to be responsive to extensive special-order requests. The usual result is a loss of efficiency with little gain in flexibility.

In sum, many managers, as well as consultants, treat both strategy and structure as part of the "art" of management rather than as elements in a science of organizations. Admittedly, what we know about organizations is far from complete, but the operating logic of forms and their inherent limits are well-known.

GROWTH AND THE LIMITS OF FIT

The basic growth strategy for each organizational form is built into its operating logic. Functionally structured, centrally planned firms grow both by penetrating new markets with their standardized goods and services and by vertically integrating those assets that can be fully utilized by the firm and that fall within its arena of competence. Diversified, decentralized firms grow by adding divisions to address new markets that fall within the scope of corporate managerial, technical, and financial know-how. Matrix firms grow along both dimensions, adding more specialists in units focused on stable markets and providing more opportunities for creating self-contained units to deal with unique contracts or markets.

Nevertheless, the current formula for growth at some point runs into problems. For example, Hewlett-Packard's computer divisions ultimately expanded into overlapping markets, creating demands for interdivisional coordination. Similarly, portions of Johnson & Johnson's formerly separate markets have now begun to combine (e.g., because of centralized purchasing of medical supplies for hospital groups and HMOs, among other reasons), presenting the possibility of scale economies in the distribution of products among subsidiary companies. At the other end of the spectrum, as specialized firms such as Wal-Mart continue to expand, demands for regional and local customization strain central planning mechanisms.

In earlier periods, long-term growth strategies tended to push most organizations toward hybrid solutions—toward some matrix of units to meet competing demands. Today, however, the pace of market change has doomed many complex mixed forms that might have worked in less turbulent times. Coordination costs, particularly the costs of time, have become too large to justify the synergistic benefits that might accrue.

Increasingly, these older growth strategies are being modified to include network features. Specialized firms can spin off regional operating subsidiaries to allow customization, often with little increase in direct operating costs because scale economies can be reached much earlier with today's technologies. At a firm such as Wal-Mart, operating units can be set up to "buy" as much customized inventory as their markets will profitably support. In a divisionalized firm, some resources can be commonly "owned" by numerous operating units, as long as they are allocated by market prices and units are free to go outside the company as needed.

In sum, large size need not be a barrier to firms whose operating logic allows resources to be allocated by market-testable decisions. Thus, large size and geographic diversity do not pose insurmountable barriers for a firm such as ABB Asea Brown Boveri, because each of its three types of autonomous operating units is guided by a well-defined market focus and bottom-line performance criteria, and all cross-buying and selling are accomplished at market prices. At General Motors, however, size and complexity do present barriers to responsiveness and efficiency, even though in an earlier era GM was hailed as a model of how to be both bigger and better. While ABB has adopted most of the features of an internal network, GM has evolved into a mixed form with no clear operating logic. It may well be that ABB's structure is not the model for General Motors. However, given the company's size and complexity, and the pace of change in its markets, it is clear that GM's current centrally coordinated structure is not a viable organizational form.

CHOOSING AMONG THE RECIPES FOR FIT

There are basically four recipes for tight fit in today's competitive environment. The right recipe for any given firm, as we have illustrated, depends on the core competence it has or believes it can develop, and where it is in its own evolution.

A FRESH START

The first recipe, available only to some firms, is to start fresh with one of the well-understood strategy-structure-process combinations. The form chosen should maximize the fit between the firm's competence and its market, and it should be thoughtfully renewed over time. Rubbermaid was not a new firm when it was transformed into a tight-fit success story, but it was not yet so large and complex that it required a massive overhaul. Its core competence could be focused on a wider market, and the structure and processes necessary to pursue its Prospector strategy could be put into place and repeated as the firm grew. Wal-Mart began with a clear Defender strategy and thoughtfully pursued a growth pattern that penetrated new markets with an increasingly efficient, centrally planned distribution system. To this point, Wal-Mart has recognized its limits and backed away from expansion moves that would take it beyond the limits of its know-how.

REDISCOVERY

The second recipe, potentially available to many large, mature firms, is to strip away accumulated layers of marginal strategic additions and structural adaptations, laying bare the core operating logic that guided them through their early success and growth. In many ways, the current level of success at Chrysler Corporation and General Electric is not the result of a new recipe but rather of the rediscovery of an earlier viable strategy-structure-process package. Chrysler's focus on innovative engineering across a limited line of products has realigned its core competence with its market. Chrysler's "new" strategy merely swept away the multimodel clutter that had obscured the clean concept with which the company began. General Electric restored an operating logic that allows it to pursue a diversification strategy carried out by autonomous units guided by clear performance criteria. Thus, it is once again assuming the fundamental organizational form it employed so profitably in the 1950s.

MODERNIZING

The third recipe, also available to many mature firms but more difficult to follow, calls for thoughtfully adding new ingredients to refurbish and enliven existing strategy-structure-process configurations that are basically sound but are not realizing the potential of the firm's underlying competence. Ford Motor Company is an example of an overly vertically integrated firm that developed new outsourcing mechanisms based on lasting, effective relationships with multiple suppliers. Outsourcing mechanisms built on trust and shared information have improved efficiency, raised quality, and shortened product development cycle times at Ford. In addition, the company makes better use of internal units, transferring ideas and designs back and forth among far-flung geographic units with the use of cross-functional, multinational teams.

The difficulty with modernizing or adding on to an existing organizational form is the same one faced by the homeowner who is seeking to remodel and expand an older house. Unless homeowner and architect have an exceptional grasp of what is needed and how to do it, old and new pieces may not fit together smoothly, and the finished house may not live up to expectations. In an organization, the mixture of old and new features must add up to one of the combinations of strategy, structure, and process whose operating logic is clear and sound.

A NETWORK ORGANIZATION

The final recipe, widely available in new industries and increasingly available in older markets, is to move fully to network structures and relationships. Of course, this recipe calls for managers to think beyond the boundaries of their own firm. Stable networks such as the one used by Nike require time and effort to be invested in developing and maintaining strong relationships with a limited number of suppliers. Dynamic networks, such as the one operated by Novell, require managers not only to think beyond their own firm to locate, and even to develop, upstream or downstream partners, but also to ensure that the firm's internal structure maximizes its ability to benefit from the combination of its own resources and those of a temporary partner. Even in internal networks, autonomously managed units must not only tend to their own performance but also facilitate the development and maintenance of sound internal market mechanisms.

CHOICES AND NON-CHOICES

The challenges posed by the network organization help to highlight both the choices that managers have and the choices they do not have in the looming twenty-first-century environment. Managers can, as we have just reiterated, choose among several recipes for fit: applying tried-and-true organizational models in carefully selected settings, rediscovering or modernizing old combinations, or fully utilizing the latest organizational approach—the network. However, managers cannot choose *not* to choose. They will find a recipe for fit or they will fail—the modern marketplace is increasingly unforgiving of poor or minimal fit.

Although managers can choose among the recipes, they cannot choose to leave out some of the ingredients. This has always been true, but never as obviously as it is in the network organization. With the functional form, managers could afford not to utilize fully the expertise of staff specialists, second-guessing or overriding their procedures. The cost of such a failure would be largely hidden in a world of weak competition. Similarly, in a divisional firm, corporate managers could restrict division operating decisions and centrally allocate some resources. In a weakly competitive industry, the loss of divisional responsiveness would be likely to go largely unnoticed.

Within a network organization, however, a manager's failure to accept all network requirements, including adopting a managerial philosophy that facilitates both full utilization of the firm's resources and effective interfirm relationships, is instantly visible. Managers who demand costly external connection procedures lower their own firm's efficiency and that of the overall network. Managers who create internal procedures that limit their firm's ability to rotate quickly to meet new demands waste both their own firm's resources and the network's options. Companies will either develop and sustain the ability to be good network partners or they will be excluded.

Perhaps most important, managers can choose how and where to invest in the continuing development of their firm's competencies, but they cannot choose not to invest. Again, this is particularly visible in the network organization. Because network firms are tightly focused on those points along the value chain where they can add the greatest value, their capabilities must be constantly renewed. Barriers to entry are typically low in network settings. A firm's know-how, its ability to apply its full resources creatively, is its primary asset, and continuous investment is the only means of guaranteeing renewal.

IDEALISM AND ECONOMICS

The recognition that managers' choices on issues of delegation and trust are becoming matters about which they have no choice is part of a much larger societal shift in which oughts are becoming musts: idealistic prescriptions have become economic rules for survival and success.

MORALE AND PRODUCTIVITY

The conflict between oughts and musts has always existed. Recall that early critics of harsh, capricious, even tyrannical treatment of employees appealed for more humane practices on moral grounds. However, those appeals really began to be heard when Henry Ford and others pointed out the enormous cost of high turnover to the efficiency of large companies. Similarly, the solicitation of employee suggestions was urged by early human relationists as being good for employee morale—an ought that could increase cooperation. However, when Joseph Scanlon demonstrated that employees' suggestions could lead to greatly reduced costs, reductions that kept some firms in business during the Depression and produced monetary rewards for employees, an ought became a must—at least within Scanlon Plan firms.

In the 1960s and 1970s, debates over issues of job enlargement and enrichment were often viewed as oughts, moral issues related primarily to the quality of work life. Today, the cross-trained employees at Southwest Air do several things well because the company depends on their ability to do them—their versatility is a key asset, not merely a morale booster. Similarly, the empowered salespeople at a Nordstrom department store are not trained and encouraged to use their initiative in meeting customers' needs in order to make salespeople happy. They are trained and encouraged because their service competence is the know-how that distinguishes Nordstrom from its competitors.

HARD AND SOFT ISSUES

In general, oughts become musts under competitive pressure. In network firms, not only is the pressure intense, the nature of the network form turns soft issues into hard issues and hard issues into soft. For example, in the mental balance sheets of most managers, people in general, and work teams in particular, tend to be carried as soft assets, while capital equipment is almost always viewed as a hard asset. This distinction is important.

Managers expect to make regular investments in hard assets and to earn a solid return on those investments. On the other hand, soft assets may be valued, but returns are uncertain and maintenance can be deferred.

In a network firm, however, the ability to flexibly and responsively apply capital equipment is just as valuable as the equipment itself. Thus, human capability becomes a hard asset in which continuing investment is acknowledged as being appropriate and from which high returns are expected. Simultaneously, while soft human assets are becoming hard, many hard physical assets, or at least the investment decisions concerning them, appear to be becoming softer. That is, while capital equipment continues to demand steady investment, the shift in network firms from scale to scope technology has broadened the array of investment options—simple linear expansions based on reliable growth forecasts are far less likely today than in the past.

This shift applies not only to current human assets but to future human assets as well. That is, to most managers, training programs to upgrade work force skills necessary to meet current and forecasted technical requirements produce hard assets for which steady investment can be easily justified. On the other hand, training beyond foreseeable needs, and educational efforts to broaden understanding of underlying industry forces, are seen at best as producing soft assets. These may have value, but value is difficult to calculate, and in competition with demands for investment in hard assets, such educational investments may well lose out.

Of course, in the rapidly evolving world of the network firm, extensive cross-training in current technology is only the starting point for human asset investment. With growing recognition that the network firm reaches its full potential only when all of its members develop a broad understanding of its technology and business requirements, formerly soft training and educational objectives become increasingly hard. When the network firm's success reflects the quality of technical and business decisions made by self-managing teams responding quickly and efficiently to myriad upstream and downstream market demands—such as in a spherical network firm—the economic payoff from educational investments becomes more visible and justifiable.

In some ways, the most important asset transition is occurring in the tradeoff between investments in control and investments in trust. Traditionally, managers have thought of control systems as hard assets, clearly necessary to ensure compliance with schedules, budgets, security procedures, and so forth. Trust, on the other hand, has been viewed by most managers as a soft asset, useful to have if available, but more of a moral condition than a substantive base for operating decisions.

Thus, while managers have generally been prepared to invest large sums in building elaborate control mechanisms to measure and "correct" the behaviors of people and processes within and between firms, investments in building trust have usually been meager and sporadic. It is clear how to build control systems and, because they are considered to be objective and hard, investments in them are seen as essential. However, it is not clear to most managers whether trust can be increased and, even if it can be, it is not clear what returns an investment in trust building will bring.

In network firms, managers are placed in positions that force them to be trusting, to take the risk that upstream and downstream partners will perform as expected—indeed, will do more than expected. As expectations are met, managers in all firms build trust that facilitates further risk taking, risk taking that lowers the costs of coupling assets among familiar partners and of locating new partners with needed resources. Moreover, managers in network firms who substitute trust for the usual methods of control build the ability to operate with "spherical" flexibility. Indeed, in network firms, normal control procedures have lost most of their "hard" objectivity. Dynamic relationships and the pace of events spotlight their weaknesses and trust becomes a necessity, worth the investment of time and money in information sharing and skill building that produces interpersonal collegiality and confidence. This is the essence of the human investment philosophy.

OUGHTS AND MUSTS: THE BROADER VIEW

The forces shaping firms and industries are also shaping national and regional economies. In many ways, the push to create networks in which firms can focus on their competencies and share resources with other firms is closely akin to the efforts shaping regional alliances such as the European Union, the North American Free Trade Agreement, and the Association of Southeast Asian Nations—the attempt to create broad arenas in which resources can be shared under market guidance without the burdensome restrictions of national boundaries and constraints. Within regional economies, international issues that historically were oughts are becoming economic musts. Indeed, negotiated agreements on common standards of environmental protection and worker rights have become key mechanisms facilitating the creation and operation of these alliances. Within each economic community, it is anticipated that member countries will pursue their own distinctive competencies, adding high value in those market areas where their resources and know-how provide them with the opportunity to make unique contributions. However, if current trade barriers are to be removed, existing advantages that are not investment-based must also be removed. That is, member countries whose product costs are lower because they do not make investments necessary to protect the environment obviously have an advantage in a common marketplace over those countries that do demand environmental protection investments. Similarly, cost advantages based on wage levels kept low by repressive national policies may also give goods from one country an advantage over those of other countries in the alliance.

When pollution and worker exploitation are debated as problems that every country "ought" to correct, progress is slow, arguments are often ignored, and competitive disadvantages can only be removed by tariffs and quotas. However, when attention to these problems is a prerequisite to full participation in a desirable marketplace, as it has been with the EU and NAFTA, countries may quickly move to meet minimal standards as a means of achieving the economic gains associated with alliance membership.

Even when such agreements address minimal standards, a firm, or even a country within a regional economy, may still have lower costs than other firms or countries, but these will be achieved through investments rather than exploitation—by creating more efficient pools of equipment and skills and more thoughtful ways of combining them.

The obvious lesson here is the same one we have been emphasizing throughout this book. In the competitive world of today and tomorrow, competencies must be investment-based. They must rest on the sustained investment of money and time, which build ever-increasing skills and know-how as well as the capability to use them to their fullest.

Within regional economies, as well as within firms and across the network organization, fit is not merely an ought, it is a must. Pieces cannot be left out; the logic of the form must be recognized and fully implemented. Wherever it is not, the economic costs to all parties are obvious. In the long run, it has probably always been the case that idealistic oughts become economic requirements. The difference today is simply that the long run is here.

A FINAL THOUGHT

We began by emphasizing that no book can give a manager the right answer to any particular organizational problem. A book can, however, help the manager to identify the right answer when he or she uncovers it. To this end, we have sought to place key organizational choices within a framework that helps clarify the options that are available, as well as the costs and benefits of each. Managers must make these choices, and they are far better able than we are to make them in their own settings.

Throughout this book, we have attempted to illustrate that while tight fit with the firm's environment and among its strategy, structure, and processes is not easy to achieve, the path to it is clear enough: Managers must understand how each of the major organizational forms works. In the onrushing new world of network organizations and the human investment philosophy we trust that managers will pursue this path, while at the same time helping one another in the search for a global economy with positive returns for all its participants.

ENDNOTES

Chapter 1. The Process of Achieving Fit

1. For a complete description of the competitive strategies described in this section, see Raymond E. Miles and Charles C. Snow, *Organizational Strategy, Structure, and Process* (New York: McGraw-Hill, 1978).
2. The literature regarding the idea that a complex organization can be made simple to its members is discussed by Danny Miller, "The Architecture of Simplicity," *Academy of Management Review* 18 (1993):116–138.
3. See Peter F. Drucker, *The Practice of Management* (New York: Harper & Row, 1954) and Thomas J. Peters and Robert H. Waterman, Jr., *In Search of Excellence: Lessons from America's Best Run Companies* (New York: Harper & Row, 1982).

Chapter 2. Early Fit: Creating New Recipes for Success

1. Our descriptions of the companies and characteristics of Period I (1880–1920) and Period II (1920–1960) are based mostly on Alfred D. Chandler, Jr., *Strategy and Structure: Chapters in the History of the American Industrial Enterprise* (Cambridge, Mass.: The M.I.T. Press, 1962).
2. The description of Carnegie Steel was adapted from Paul R. Lawrence and Davis Dyer, *Renewing American Industry* (New York: Free Press, 1983), chapter 3.
3. See Frederick W. Taylor, *The Principles of Scientific Management* (New York: Harper & Brothers, 1911).
4. The description of General Motors was adapted from Chandler, op. cit., chapter 3. See also Alfred P. Sloan, Jr., *My Years with General Motors* (New York: Macfadden, 1965) and Albert Lee, *Call Me Roger* (Chicago: Contemporary Books, 1988).
5. The description of Sears, Roebuck was adapted from Chandler, op. cit., chapter 5 and from Drucker, op. cit., chapter 4.
6. See Drucker, op. cit., chapter 11.
7. The description of TRW Systems was adapted from Stanley M. Davis and Paul R. Lawrence, *Matrix* (Reading, Mass.: Addison-Wesley, 1977), 91–101.

8. For a complete description of the managerial ideologies discussed in this section, see Raymond E. Miles, *Theories of Management: Implications for Organizational Behavior and Development* (New York: McGraw-Hill, 1975).

Chapter 3. The Modern Transition

1. The description of Wal-Mart was adapted from a Special Report appearing in *Business Month*, December 1988, pp. 38 and 42.

2. The description of Rubbermaid was adapted from a Special Report appearing in *Business Month*, December 1988, pp. 38 and 42, and from Alan Farnham, "America's Most Admired Company," *Fortune*, February 7, 1994, 50–54.

3. The description of Chrysler Corporation was adapted from James Brian Quinn, *Chrysler Corporation* (copyrighted case, The Amos Tuck School of Business Administration, Dartmouth College, 1977).

4. The description of General Electric was adapted from Noel Tichy and Ram Charan, "Speed, Simplicity, Self-Confidence: An Interview with Jack Welch," *Harvard Business Review* (September–October 1989):112–120; and from Thomas W. Malnight, "GE—Preparing for the 1990s," Harvard Business School Case #9-390-091, 1989 (revised October 14, 1990).

5. Russell L. Ackoff, "Corporate Perestroika: The Internal Market Economy," in William E. Halal, Ali Geranmayeh, and John Pourdehnad, eds., *Internal Markets: Bringing the Power of Free Enterprise Inside Your Organization* (New York: Wiley, 1993), 15–26.

6. For a complete description of stable, dynamic, and internal networks, see Charles C. Snow, Raymond E. Miles, and Henry J. Coleman, Jr., "Managing 21st Century Network Organizations," *Organizational Dynamics* (Winter 1992):5–20.

7. For discussions of the organizational aspects of Japanese *keiretsu*, see Charles H. Ferguson, "Computers and the Coming of the U.S. Keiretsu," *Harvard Business Review* (July-August 1990): 55–70; "Learning From Japan," *Business Week*, January 27, 1992, 52–60; and "Japan: All in the Family," *Newsweek*, June 10, 1991, 37–40.

Chapter 5. Failure to Respond to External Change

1. The description of American Brands and other tobacco companies was adapted from Robert H. Miles, *Coffin Nails and Corporate Strategies* (Englewood Cliffs, N.J.: Prentice-Hall, 1980).

2. See Charles C. Snow and Lawrence G. Hrebiniak, "Strategy, Distinctive Competence, and Organizational Performance," *Administrative Science Quarterly* 25 (June 1980): 317–336.

3. This section is based on descriptions in Robert A. Pitts and Charles C. Snow, *Strategies for Competitive Success* (New York: Wiley, 1986).

4. For an interesting discussion of the downward spiral of companies that went bankrupt, see Donald C. Hambrick and Richard D'Aveni, "Large Corporate Failures as Downward Spirals," *Administrative Science Quarterly* 33 (1988): 1–23.
5. See Miles and Snow, op. cit., chapter 9.
6. For a discussion of ways to avoid the so-called Abilene paradox, see Jerry B. Harvey, "The Abilene Paradox: The Management of Agreement," *Organizational Dynamics* 3 (Summer 1974): 63–80.
7. For discussions of the "outsider" phenomenon, see Brian Dumaine, "What's So Hot About Outsiders?", *Fortune*, November 29, 1993, 63–67, and "CEOs with the Outside Edge: Why They're in, as Never Before," *Business Week*, October 11, 1993, 60–62.

Chapter 6. Unraveling From Within

1. We first introduced the concept of internal unraveling through extension and modification failures in Raymond E. Miles and Charles C. Snow, "Causes of Failure in Network Organizations," *California Management Review* 34 (Summer 1992): 53–72.

Chapter 7. The Network Organization

1. In our early work, we discussed how market forces could be injected into traditional organizational structures to make them more efficient and responsive (Miles and Snow, *Organizational Strategy, Structure, and Process*, op. cit., chapter 9). Subsequent publications extended market concepts to internal work teams (Raymond E. Miles and Howard R. Rosenberg, "The Human Resources Approach to Management: Second-Generation Issues," *Organizational Dynamics* (Winter 1982): 26–41), as well as to external groups, which we called "dynamic networks" (Raymond E. Miles and Charles C. Snow, "Fit, Failure, and the Hall of Fame," *California Management Review* (Spring, 1984): 10–28). As network organizations became more plentiful in the 1980s, it was possible to describe them in more detail (Raymond E. Miles and Charles C. Snow, "Network Organizations: New Concepts for New Forms," *California Management Review* (Spring 1986): 62–73; Hans Thorelli, "Networks: Between Markets and Hierarchies," *Strategic Management Journal* (January-February 1986): 37–52.

The network form of organization gained wide visibility after it was the subject of a *Business Week* cover story in 1986 ("The Hollow Corporation," March 3, 1986). This story sparked a debate in the business press about the merits and drawbacks of networks (see, for example, a series of articles by Christopher Lorenz in *The Financial Times* in the late 1980s).

By the end of the 1980s, network organizations in their various forms were a fact of organizational life. A virtual explosion of books and articles explored—and generally endorsed—strategic alliances, value-adding partnerships, and other types of network structures. In general, network organizations were seen as a powerful tool for American and foreign firms to strengthen their positions in the global economy. Most notable among these writings were William E. Halal, *The New Capitalism* (New York: Wiley, 1986); Russell Johnston and Paul R. Lawrence, "Beyond Vertical Integration—The Rise of the Value-Adding Partnership," *Harvard Business Review* (1988); Peter F. Drucker, *The New Realities* (New York: Harper & Row, 1989); Rosabeth Moss Kanter, *When Giants Learn to Dance* (New York: Simon and Schuster, 1989); Charles Handy, *The Age of Unreason* (Boston: Harvard Business School Press, 1990); Walter W. Powell, "Neither Market Nor Hierarchy: Network Forms of Organization," in Barry M. Staw and Larry L. Cummings, eds., *Research in Organizational Behavior*, vol. 12 (Greenwich, Conn.: JAI Press, 1990), 295–336; and Robert B. Reich, *The Work of Nations* (New York: Alfred A. Knopf, 1991).

2. For discussions of the Italian experience, see G. Becattini, "Italian Industrial Districts: Problems and Perspectives," *International Studies of Management and Organization* 21 (1991): 83–90; S. Brusco, "The Emilian Model: Productive Decentralisation and Social Integration," *Cambridge Journal of Economics* 6 (1982): 167–184; Giorgio Inzerilli, "The Italian Alternative: Flexible Organization and Social Management," *International Studies of Management and Organization* 20 (1990): 6–21; and Martin Piore and Charles Sabel, *The Second Industrial Divide: Prospects for Prosperity* (New York: Basic Books, 1984).

3. See Richard Gordon, "Structural Change, Strategic Alliances and the Spatial Reorganization of Silicon Valley's Semiconductor Industry," in Denis Maillat, Michel Quevit, and Lanfranco Senn, eds., *Reseaux d'Innovation et Milieux Innovateurs: Un Pari Pour le Developpement Regional* (Neuchatel, Switzerland: Université de Neuchatel, 1993), 51–71. See also AnnaLee Saxenian, "Regional Networks and the Resurgence of Silicon Valley," *California Management Review* (Fall 1990): 89–112. For a comparison of the organizational experiences in Silicon Valley and Boston's Route 128, see AnnaLee Saxenian, *Regional Networks: Industrial Adaptation in Silicon Valley and Route 128* (Cambridge, Mass.: Harvard University Press, 1994).

4. For an overview of this process, see "What Big Companies Can Learn," *Business Week*, Special Issue on Enterprise, 1993, 190–257.

5. The description of Nike was adapted from Donald Katz, "Triumph of the Swoosh," *Sports Illustrated*, September 1993, 54–73; company annual reports and Form 10-K; and Nena Baker, "The Hidden Hands of Nike: The Human Story Behind the Profits Afforded by Cheap Asian Labor," *The Sunday Oregonian*, August 9, 1992.

6. Dynamic networks have also been called "modular" organizations. See Shawn Tully, "The Modular Corporation," *Fortune*, February 8, 1993, 106–114.

7. The description of Dell Computer Corporation was adapted from company annual reports; Tully, op. cit.; and Jim Emerson, "No-Cost Expansion," *D&B Reports* (March-April 1993): 54.

8. The description of Novell Inc. was adapted from David B. Yoffie, *Strategic Management in Information Technology* (Englewood Cliffs, N.J.: Prentice-Hall, 1994); " 'The Industry Needs an Alternative'— But Will It Be Novell?", *Business Week*, February 1, 1993, 69–70; and "Novell: End of an Era?", *Business Week*, November 22, 1993, 93–95.

9. *Business Week* used the term "hollow corporation" pejoratively in its March 3, 1986, cover story. However, recognizing that thoughtful outsourcing does not necessarily cause a company to lose its distinctive competence, other authors have discussed how firms are "learning to love the hollow corporation." See James Brian Quinn, Thomas L. Doorley, and Penny C. Paquette, "Technology in Services: Rethinking Strategic Focus," *Sloan Management Review* 31 (Winter 1990): 83.

10. The description of ABB Asea Brown Boveri was adapted from William Taylor, "The Logic of Global Business: An Interview with ABB's Percy Barnevik," *Harvard Business Review* (March-April 1991): 91–105. See also Tom Peters, *Liberation Management: Necessary Disorganization for the Nanosecond Nineties* (New York: Alfred A. Knopf, 1992), chapter 4.

11. See William E. Halal, Ali Geranmayeh, and John Pourdehnad, *Internal Markets: Bringing the Power of Free Enterprise Inside Your Organization* (New York: Wiley, 1993).

12. For discussions of the modular corporation, see Tully, op. cit.; the virtual corporation, see William H. Davidow and Michael S. Malone, *The Virtual Corporation* (New York: Harper Business, 1992); and the horizontal corporation, see "The Horizontal Corporation," *Business Week*, December 20, 1993, 76–81.

Chapter 8. Triple Fit: Network Roles and the Spherical Form

1. An earlier description of these roles can be found in Snow, Miles, and Coleman, op. cit. An in-depth study of these roles in three health care networks can be found in Charles C. Snow and James

B. Thomas, "Building Networks: Broker Roles and Behavior," in Peter Lorange, Bala Chakravarthy, Johan Roos, and Andrew Van de Ven, eds., *Implementing Strategic Processes: Change, Learning, and Cooperation* (Oxford, England: Basil Blackwell, 1993), 217–238.

2.   Vincenzo Perrone, presentation made at a symposium of the Academy of Management, Las Vegas, Nev., August 1992.

3.   For examples of different kinds of self-managing teams, see Charles C. Manz and Henry P. Sims, Jr., *Business Without Bosses: How Self-Managing Teams Are Building High-Performing Companies* (New York: Wiley, 1993).

4.   The description of Technical and Computer Graphics was adapted from John Mathews, *TCG: Sustainable Economic Organisation Through Networking* (Kensington, Australia: Industrial Relations Research Centre, The University of New South Wales, 1992).

5.   For an early example of this phenomenon, see Miles and Rosenberg, op. cit.

6.   See Grant Miles, Charles C. Snow, and Mark P. Sharfman, "Industry Variety and Performance," *Strategic Management Journal* 14 (March 1993): 163–177.

Chapter 9.   A New Managerial Philosophy: The Human Investment Model

1.   The phrase human investment philosophy, as well as a description of the philosophy's main characteristics, first appeared in Raymond E. Miles and W.E. Douglas Creed, "Organizational Forms and Managerial Philosophies" (working paper, University of California, Berkeley, 1992).

2.   The relationship between organizational form and managerial philosophy was initially explored by Alan D. Meyer, "Adapting to Environmental Jolts," *Administrative Science Quarterly* 27 (December 1982): 515–536.

3.   See *The Lincoln Electric Company*, Harvard Business School Case #376-028, 1975.

4.   James F. Lincoln, *Incentive Management: A New Approach to Human Relationships in Industry and Business* (Cleveland, Ohio: The Lincoln Electric Company, 1951).

5.   See Gordon E. Forward, Dennis E. Beach, David A. Gray, and James C. Quick, "Mentofacturing: A Vision for American Industrial Excellence," *The Academy of Management Executive* 5 (August 1991): 32–44.

6.   See John W. Kensinger and John D. Martin, "Financing Network Organizations," *Journal of Applied Corporate Finance* (Spring 1991): 66–76.

7.   Ibid.

Chapter 10.   The Process of Corporate Redesign

1. See Edward E. Lawler III, Susan Albers Mohrman, and Gerald E. Ledford, Jr., *Employee Involvement and Total Quality Management* (San Francisco: Jossey-Bass, 1992).

2. See Michael Hammer and James Champy, *Reengineering the Corporation: A Manifesto for Business Revolution* (New York: HarperBusiness, 1993).

3. See Tracy Goss, Richard Pascale, and Anthony Athos, "The Reinvention Roller Coaster: Risking the Present for a Powerful Future," *Harvard Business Review* (November-December 1993): 97–108.

4. See Michael L. Tushman, William H. Newman, and Elaine Romanelli, "Convergence and Upheaval: Managing the Unsteady Pace of Organizational Evolution," *California Management Review* (Fall 1986): 29–44.

5. See Richard Cyert and James G. March, *A Behavioral Theory of the Firm* (Englewood Cliffs, N.J.: Prentice-Hall, 1963).

6. See James Brian Quinn, *Strategies for Change: Logical Incrementalism* (Homewood, Ill.: Irwin, 1980).

7. For a discussion of the changes made at Xerox, see David T. Kearns and David A. Nadler, *Prophets in the Dark: How Xerox Reinvented Itself and Beat Back the Japanese* (New York: HarperCollins, 1992).

Chapter 11.   The Self-Renewing Organization: Learning and Teaching Adaptation

1. Reported in Peter B. Vaill, *Managing as a Performing Art: New Ideas for a World of Chaotic Change* (San Francisco: Jossey-Bass, 1989), chapter 1.

2. There are numerous descriptions of the learning organization. Three of the most popular are Ikujiro Nonaka, "The Knowledge-Creating Company," *Harvard Business Review* (November-December 1991): 96–104; Peter M. Senge, *The Fifth Discipline: The Art and Practice of the Learning Organization* (New York: Doubleday/Currency, 1990); and James Brian Quinn, *Intelligent Enterprise: A Knowledge and Service Based Paradigm for Industry* (New York: Free Press, 1992). For a review of the academic literature on the learning organization, see George P. Huber, "Organizational Learning: The Contributing Processes and the Literatures," *Organization Science* 2 (1991): 88–115.

3. David J. Teece, Gary Pisano, and Amy Shuen, "Dynamic Capabilities and Strategic Management," Working Paper, University of California, Berkeley, 1992.

4. Lincoln, op. cit.

5. Chris Argyris and Donald Schon, *Organizational Learning: A Theory-in-Action Perspective* (Reading, Mass.: Addison-Wesley, 1978).
6. See Tom Peters, *Thriving on Chaos: Handbook for a Managerial Revolution* (New York: Alfred A. Knopf, 1987).
7. See Farnham, op. cit.
8. See Ricardo Semler, "Managing Without Managers: How One Unorthodox Company Makes Money by Avoiding Decisions, Rules, and Executive Authority," *Harvard Business Review* (September-October 1989): 73–83. For a more complete description of Semco, see Ricardo Semler, *Maverick!* (London: Century, 1993).
9. Reported in Donald Katz, op. cit.
10. See, for example, "Motorola: Training for the Millennium," *Business Week*, March 28, 1994, 158–161.

ACKNOWLEDGMENTS

We wish to acknowledge the contributions of four individuals who helped make our book more interesting, substantive, and readable. Gordon Holbein aided in the book's conceptualization and located many useful company examples. Douglas Creed helped us to understand and describe the managerial philosophy required by tomorrow's organizations. Shelley Gordon improved the manuscript in numerous ways—mainly by pushing us to be clear, accurate, and informative. Peggy Simcic Brønn's communications expertise, as well as her keen editorial eye, was of immense value in polishing the final manuscript. To each of these people, thank you for your help.

The publishing team at the Free Press was conscientious, friendly, and very professional. We wish to express our appreciation to Robert Wallace, Elena Vega, and Celia Knight for making the publishing process go so smoothly.

INDEX

A&P, 19
ABB Asea Brown Boveri, 17, 60,
    112–15, 127, 190
Ackoff, Russell, 57, 128
Adidas, 104
Alcoa, 116
Allaire, Paul, 165
American Brands, 70–72, 76, 78
American Express, 52
AT&T, 17, 73, 100, 180
American West, 180
Analyzer (see Strategy)
Apple Computer, 108

Barkley, Charles, 103
Barriers, to strategic change
    downward spiral, 79–80
    managerial ideology, 79
    market leadership, 77–78
    strategic predisposition, 75–
        77
Benetton, 99
Blue Cross/Blue Shield, 116
BMW, 104
Boeing, 138

Canadian Pacific, 86–87
Canon, 166
Capability, dynamic, 171
Carnegie, Andrew, 26
Carnegie Steel, 8, 26–29, 48

Chaparral Steel, 182
Chrysler Corporation, 17, 45,
    52–53, 71, 164–67, 191–
        92
Citibank, 36
Clark Equipment, 116
Compaq Computer, 108
Control Data Corporation, 116
Cordiner, Ralph, 39
Coopetition, 110
Corning, 104, 175, 185
Corporation
    horizontal, 117
    modular, 116
    virtual, 116–17, 130

Daimler-Benz, 100
Defender (see Strategy)
Dell Computer Corporation, 17,
    57, 108–11, 118, 126
Digital Equipment Corporation,
    36, 108
Doering, Otto, 31
Drucker, Peter, 21, 32, 90
DuPont Chemical Company, 32,
    87
DuPont, Pierre, 30
Durant, William, 29–30

Eastern Airlines, 70
Eastman Kodak, 161–62

Failure, organizational
  extension mistakes, 83–93
  modification mistakes, 83–93
  process of, 65–69
Fit, organizational
  articulation of, 20–22
  dynamics of, 18–20
  early, 12, 23–24
  external, 11–15, 70–82
  fragility of, 67–68
  internal, 11, 15–18
  minimal, 12, 19
  recipes for, 191–93
  tight, 12, 19–20, 187–90
  unraveling of, 83–93
Ford, Henry, 27–28, 71, 79, 195
Ford Motor Company, 27–30, 48,
    70–71, 76, 84–86, 192
Form, organizational
  divisional, 15–16, 29–34, 39–40,
    50–51, 87–89, 188–90, 194
  functional, 15–16, 26–28, 38–39,
    48–50, 84–87, 188–90,
    193–94
  matrix, 16, 34–37, 40–41, 89
  network, 15–16, 56–57, 60–62,
    95–120, 137–40, 190,
    193–94, 196–200
    dynamic, 59, 106–112, 126–27
    internal, 60, 112–16, 127–28
    spherical, 128–40
    stable, 59–60, 101–106,
      125–26
F. W. Woolworth Co., 31

Gault, Stanley, 178
General Electric, 8, 39, 45, 54–56,
    84, 90–92, 100, 155, 159,
    166–67, 178–79, 191–92

General Mills, 87
General Motors, 3–4, 8, 14, 17,
    20–21, 29–34, 39, 52, 54, 71,
    82, 88, 90, 159, 190

Hall of Fame, corporate, 7–8
Harley-Davidson, 45, 52–54, 86,
    166–67
Hewlett-Packard, 12, 22, 32–34,
    172, 175, 183, 189
Hewlett, William, 33

IBM, 16, 20, 36, 52, 57, 70, 73–76,
    78, 82, 100, 108, 159
Industrial Light and Magic, 127
Intel Corporation, 14, 57, 108,
    173

Jackson, Bo, 103
J.C. Penney, 31
Johnson & Johnson, 155, 172–75,
    180–81, 185, 189
Jordan, Michael, 103

Kearns, David, 165
Keiretsu, 59, 117

Lewis Galoob Toys, 59, 126
Liggett & Meyers, 70, 77
Lincoln Electric Company, 154,
    173, 178, 181
Lincoln, James F., 154, 173

Management by committee,
    36–37
Management by exception, 28
Management by objectives, 32

Matsushita Industrial Electric
    Corporation, 14, 36
McDonnell-Douglas, 89, 138
Microsoft Corporation, 165
Minnesota Mining and Manufac-
    turing (3M), 136–37, 160,
    172, 178–80, 182
Mirer, Rick, 103
Misfit, organizational, 18–19, 65–69
Mitsubishi Electric, 100
Montgomery Ward, 31
Motorola, 104, 156, 183
Mourning, Alonzo, 103

National Semiconductor, 13–14
Nike Inc., 17, 59–60, 102–105, 118,
    125–26, 181–82, 193
Nissan Motor, 100
Noorda, Raymond, 110
Nordstrom's, 130, 195
Novell Inc., 109–10, 112, 126, 156,
    193

Operating logic
    definition of, 37–38
    of the divisional organization,
        39–40
    of the functional organization,
        38–39
    of the matrix organization,
        40–41
Organization
    learning, 170, 175–76
    teaching, 170, 176–78

Packard, David, 33
Pan American Airlines, 70, 80
Penn Central, 19
People's Express, 19

Perestroika, corporate, 57, 128
Perrone, Vincenzo, 131
Peters, Tom, 21, 176
Philip Morris, 72, 78, 100
Philips Electronics, 36
Philosophy, managerial
    as a barrier to fit or change, 22
    definition of, 142
    Human Investment, 141–56
    Human Relations, 41–43
    Human Resources, 41–43
    Traditional, 41–43
Process reengineering, 159
Procter & Gamble, 36, 160, 172
Prospector (see Strategy)

Raytheon, 89
Reactor (see Strategy)
Redesign, organizational, 159–
    68
Reebok, 104
Reinvention, organizational, 159
Renewal, organizational
    and dynamic capability, 182–83
    and performance criteria,
        178–79
    and rewards, 179–82
    in network firms, 183–84
    process of, 173–75
R. J. Reynolds, 72, 78
Roles, management
    designer/architect, 122–23
    nurturer/developer, 124
    process engineer/co-operator,
        123–24
Rosenwald, Julius, 31
Rubbermaid Corporation, 2–4, 8,
    16, 44–45, 50–51, 56, 84,
    90–91, 178–80, 183

Sears, Richard, 31
Sears, Roebuck, 3–4, 21, 39, 52, 54,
    87, 90, 159
Simplicity, organizational, 20–
    21
Scanlon, Joseph, 195
Scanlon Plan, 195
Semco, 180
Sloan, Alfred, 30, 39
Southwest Air, 182–83, 195
Standard Oil of New Jersey, 32
Strategy, competitive
    Analyzer, 14–16, 40, 72, 76, 81
    Defender, 12–17, 38–39, 72, 76,
        80–81, 90, 172, 191
    Prospector, 12–14, 39, 72,
        75–76, 81, 172, 191
Structure (see Form)
Sun Microsystems, 165

Taylor, Frederick, 28
Teams, self-managing, 130–31,
    136–37
Technical and Computer Graph-
    ics, 132–35

Teece, David, 171
Texas Instruments, 36
Total Quality Management, 159
Triangulation, 132–34
TRW Corporation, 8, 34–36, 89
UniDirect Corporation, 109
Unilever, 89
U.S. Steel (USX), 26

Volkswagen, 100

Wal-Mart, 2–4, 8, 14, 16, 44–45,
    48–50, 56, 84, 90–91, 190–91
Wang Laboratories, 19
Waterman, Robert, 21
Welch, Jack, 55
Westinghouse Electric Corpora-
    tion, 52, 100
Wood, Robert, 31–32, 39
Woolworth's (see F. W. Wool-
    worth Co.)
Workforce Solutions, 57

Xerox Corporation, 109, 136,
    164–67

RAYMOND E. MILES is Trefethen Professor of Organizational Behavior and former dean of the Haas School of Business Administration at the University of California, Berkeley. CHARLES C. SNOW is Professor of Business Administration at Pennsylvania State University and a frequent lecturer in executive development programs throughout the world.